understanding your

dog

understanding your
dog

Understanding and training your dog for life

Erica Peachey

This is a Parragon Publishing Book
This edition published in 2003

Parragon Publishing
Queen Street House
4 Queen Street
Bath BA1 1HE, UK

Created and produced for Parragon by
The Bridgewater Book Company Ltd.

Creative Director Stephen Knowlden
Art Director Michael Whitehead
Editorial Director Fiona Biggs
Project Editor Sarah Bragginton
Designer Tony Truscott
Studio Manager Chris Morris
Index completed by Indexing Specialists

ISBN: 1-40540-733-6

Printed in China

contents

introduction

A dog is man's best friend, but are we a best friend to the dog? We are dog owners, probably dog lovers, but how well do we understand them? Some people feel that their dog "understands every word they say", but how many of us have made the same effort to understand what our dogs are saying to us?

Our dogs today bear little resemblance to their ancestors, the wolves. Man has intervened and produced the wide variety of breeds we have today. The popularity of pets means that many dogs are wanted as companions. But being a pet requires a huge range of skills and the ability to adapt and learn far more than many working dogs.

When we take on our new puppy or dog, it is likely that we want him to be a family pet, who will share our lives for perhaps 12 or 15 years. Therefore, we must put effort into insuring that this is the case, and invest time now to enable us to enjoy our dog more fully in the years to come.

Preparing him for life is vital, and this includes socializing and teaching him what it is we want.

So many aspects of our lives are now focused on work that we often forget since the importance of fun and games. However, these are at least as important to our dog as they are to us.

This book covers these topics and more, the aim being to help owners better understand their own dogs. It will not answer every question that may arise—the understanding of dogs and their behavior is a huge and often complex area—but it will provide pointers to finding the answers to more specific queries.

This is a complex subject and only a small cross section can be covered in a book. It is strongly recommended that owners continue to expand their knowledge by doing the following things:
- watching their dog
- adapting advice to insure suitability for their own dog
- finding out about dog-training clubs
- seeking appropriate help if serious problems have arisen.

As I write this book, my own two dogs are lying fast asleep, one by my feet, the other by my side. They look perfectly relaxed, but I know that as soon as I consider moving from my desk, they will raise their heads and watch. If I move, they are likely to follow me, especially if there is a chance I may be doing something important, such as going into the kitchen to fetch my shoes for a walk. Life with our dogs can be wonderful. It is up to us to insure that it is.

Life Skills

The importance of training

Many restrictions are placed on our dogs today, so it is essential that we have some degree of control over them, especially when we take them out and about. Therefore, training for life is something we must teach. Sometimes, however, problems do arise. Where possible, these should be prevented, as prevention is so much easier than cure, but there are steps that can be taken to resolve any difficulties.

Understanding our dog is important if we are to have a good relationship with our pets.
Remember—dogs are not like humans, however much we want them to be.

meet ben

Ben lives in a rescue kennels; he is a big handsome dog, with a wagging tail. He hasn't always lived here—he used to have a family.

Ben was the result of an accidental mating. His mother escaped while in season and met with the local canine "Romeo." Ben and his eight brothers and sisters were the result. They were advertised as "free to a good home" and Mrs. White took her two young children to look at them, having become tired of their constant demands for a dog, and feeling that maybe a dog would teach them about responsibility. They chose Ben because of his unusual coloring, and proudly took him home. Ben happily played with the children, but no one taught him the rules of the games, and so the children became wary of him as he became bigger and rougher. Games were no fun for the children, so Ben was excluded from them. He chewed the children's toys, so he was shut in the kitchen. Bored, lonely and confused, Ben chewed the kitchen cabinets, so he was put outside in a kennel. Whenever anyone went out into the garden, Ben was so pleased to see them that he jumped all over them. After knocking over a few neighboring children, Ben earned a reputation as a dangerous dog, and his owners kept him tied up.

Mrs. White took him for walks. At first, they walked around the street, but when he became too strong and almost pulled Mrs. White into the road, she began taking him in the car to a local field, populated by dog walkers. Ben became difficult to catch because he would rather play with the other dogs, so Mrs. White could only take him at weekends, when she had more time. Other dog owners began complaining about Ben because his "games" were too rough, so Mrs. White decided that he did not deserve a walk if he could not behave himself.

Life continued like this for a while, until neighbors made a formal complaint to the authorities about Ben's constant barking in the garden. The children had lost interest long ago, preferring their computer games, and Mrs. White felt that she had done all she could for Ben. He was no pleasure to own, and cost a great deal to feed. She took him to the local animal rescue. Poor Ben was alone and confused. His "resumé" did not make impressive reading—"destructive in the house, not safe with children, over-boisterous and aggressive to other dogs." Even those people attracted to his friendly face were put off when they heard his history. And so there he stays. Most of the staff like him, even though he is "a handful."

There are so many "Bens" around who are at some stage in this story. Some have happy endings, some do not. With preparation and understanding, many of these difficulties can be avoided and our dogs can share and enjoy life with us.

Throughout the book, the dog is referred to as "he." This is purely for ease of reading—exactly the same applies to male and female dogs except where stated otherwise.

Sadly, many dogs who are seen to be "difficult" end up in a local animal rescue. This sad fate can be avoided with a little care and attention.

understanding a dog's basic nature

1

When we look at our dog, what do we see? Brown eyes, wagging tail, cold nose? But what is going on beneath the surface? What would it be like to be a dog? Of course, we cannot know, but the more we understand about our dog, the better we can appreciate why he does what he does—what instincts he has, what his senses tell him, what a wagging tail means. Looking at our pet, it is sometimes hard to remember that he is descended from the wolves. Selective breeding over many generations has produced many changes. Different needs have given rise to a wide variety of breeds and types, and now the dogs we meet are as varied as the uses we have for them. To be a companion or working dog, guard or rescue dog, to protect or to hunt—our dogs adapt to all these roles.

the origins of modern dogs
comparisons with wolves

Where do dogs come from?

It seems most likely that our domestic dog is evolved from the wolf and that the process started around 14,000 years ago. Why? We can only guess. Maybe the wolf decided that it was in his best interests to come closer to human encampments, where he would have access to leftovers and remains. Maybe human beings decided that it was good to have the wolves around, as security from other predators. Wolves could run faster than humans, so teamwork between dog and human meant increased efficiency in hunting. Both benefited from this alliance, and early humans developed their own breeding programe. Nervous, aggressive, or independent wolves would not be selected as breeding stock. The friendliest puppies were chosen and protected, and human association with the dog began.

Through recent studies with foxes, it has been found that breeding for behavioral traits also affects physical characteristics. After a few generations of selective breeding, the foxes were retaining their juvenile characteristics, such as a domed head and big eyes. Since we have strongly influenced the breeding of dogs through many generations, we have made substantial

Some breeds of dog resemble the wolf more closely than others...

... but all share a high proportion of instincts with their wild relatives.

alterations from the basic model of the wolf. It is these changes that have enabled the dog to become the successful pet that he is. Physically, we have changed the wolf to suit our purposes. When looking at a German Shepherd Dog or Siberian Husky, we can see some similarities, but compare the Dachshund, the Old English Sheepdog or the Great Dane and it is hard to find many resemblances.

Some of the changes include:
Eye color: many wolves have striking light colored eyes. When a wolf looks at you, you know about it. Most dogs have brown eyes.

Noise: wolves rarely bark, but barking is one of the features that humans have selected. Wolves howl to

Contrary to popular opinion, wolves are not highly aggressive toward each other. A stable pack exists around a well-defined hierarchy, which allows the wolves to co-operate with each other. It would not be in the best interests of the pack for members to harm each other.

communicate with each other. Domestic dogs tend to howl less, but they have a whole range of other vocalizations, including barking and whining.

Breed differences: almost every attribute has been manipulated and altered by human intervention. Ears may be floppy or erect, coats may be extremely short or long, with every variation in between. Some dogs can raise their hackles to communicate, some can't. Some tails are naturally carried high, others low, and some are removed altogether. Somehow, through all the changes, dogs are expected to be able to read each other's signals. The amazing thing is that in most instances, they do! Behaviorally, too, there have been many changes. Whereas a wolf would not make a suitable pet, there are now many varieties of dog around whose traits have been adapted for a variety of situations.

However, we can learn a great deal though watching wolves and their behavior. They are pack animals, they hunt in a group, and they conform to rules within their group. Pack leadership is not maintained through aggression. In fact true aggression is very much a last resort. Stability is maintained by subtle signals between the leader and the rest of the pack. It is not so much that he

Our dogs adapt to a wide variety of situations and can become valued members of the family, sharing life with us for many years.

demands first access to any food, it is more that the others step back to give him this privilege. He does not push past anyone, they all stand back to allow him to pass. If any sort of confrontation is needed, clear body signals are usually sufficient to defuse the situation.

Wolves are beautiful to look at and fascinating to study, but they are not pets. They are wild animals, predators adapted for survival.

Essential differences

Differences between Dogs and Wolves
- dogs are far less suspicious and nervous than wolves
- dogs are much more adaptable and cope with change more readily
- dogs are able to be house-broken
- dogs can form close bonds with people
- dogs are more responsive
- dogs are more able to cope with the presence of people and other animals without responding aggressively

different **breeds**

Through our long association with the dog, we have initiated almost every change imaginable. Some of these changes have been selected through necessity, such as to help man with a certain type of work, others purely in the interests of fashion and style. Some are of benefit to the dog, some are certainly not.

The English Kennel club has divided dogs into several different groups.

The Pastoral Group. This includes the herding dogs, bred to help man control and look after stock. These dogs are generally active, playful, like to chase and are relatively easy to train for the work they are asked to undertake.

The Gundog Group. Originally bred to find and retrieve game, this group includes the retrievers, setters and spaniels. They are bred to work closely with man, to be sociable and, usually, to have a good retrieving instinct.

The Terrier Group. These dogs were originally bred to do a job that normally involved killing. Therefore, they are often more independent, and extremely brave and tough.

As well as finding out what the breed was originally bred for, look at the breeder of your puppy. What are they breeding for—show dogs, working dogs, or dogs to be good pets?

A cute puppy, but what was he bred to do?

When a dog is down a hole he has to make his own decisions, not wait to be told. Selective breeding has meant that most terriers are good pets with strong characters.

The Toy Dog Group. Most dogs in this group were bred to be companions or lap dogs. They are generally friendly and make affectionate pets.

Bred to withstand the climate in their native Hungary, the Puli's coat is wonderful to look at but involves a great deal of care.

The Working Group. Many of these dogs were originally bred to guard and search, perhaps developed to protect man or livestock. There are also dogs developed to pull carts, boats, or sleighs, as well as to search and rescue.

The Hound Group. This includes the dogs who hunt by sight and those who use their sense of smell. Many of these dogs have been bred to hunt in packs, and these breeds in particular are very independent and often like to run and do their own thing.

Popular throughout the world, the German Shepherd Dog has been used for many years as a working dog as well as a companion.

Large or small, long coated or short, there are dogs to suit all requirements.

The Utility Group. These are breeds that do not fit into any of the other categories. All have been bred for some purpose, but these vary considerably and therefore the dogs within this group are extremely varied.

These groups do not cover all dogs. There are other types that are not officially recognized by the English Kennel Club at this time. Some of these are discussed later.

popular **dog breeds**

According to the English Kennel Club, the most popular pedigree dogs in 1999 were:

NAME	POSSIBLE ORIGINS OF BREED	GROUP	GENERAL TRAITS
01. Labrador Retriever	possibly originally bred to retrieve fish	Gundog	Very sociable, can be boisterous
02. German Shepherd Dog (Alsatian)	guarding and driving sheep, now bred for many functions	Pastoral	Possibly the most popular breed worldwide
03. West Highland White	hunting vermin	Terrier	Energetic, independent, brave
04. Cocker Spaniel	to flush woodcock	Gundog	Usually a fun family dog
05. Golden Retriever	to retrieve game	Gundog	Generally a great family dog
06. English Springer Spaniel	to flush game birds	Gundog	Can be extremely lively, especially if bred from working stock
07. Cavalier King Charles Spaniel	companion	Toy	A lovely, gentle companion
08. Staffordshire Bull Terrier	historic connection with fighting	Terrier	Lots of character, strength, determination and fun
09. Boxer	guarding and fighting	Working	Energetic, with a great sense of humor
10. Yorkshire Terrier	unknown	Toy	Small, adaptable, fun
11. Rottweiler	hunting wild boar	Working	A strong dog with a strong character
12. Border Terrier	going to ground in search of fox	Terrier	A happy, friendly, companion dog
13. Shih Tzu	from China	Utility	Usually outgoing
14. Lhasa Apso	guarding Tibetan monasteries	Utility	Can be independent
15. Dobermann	named after its German breeder	Working	Strong and active
16. Dalmatian	to accompany carriages	Utility	Active, agile and strong
17. Bull Terrier	bull baiting	Terrier	A strong dog full of character and fun
18. Bichon Frise	companion dog	Toy	Affectionate and friendly
19. Weimaraner	hunt, point, retrieve	Gundog	Energetic, can be strongwilled
20. Miniature Schnauzer	coachman's dog	Utility	Active and quick to learn

(list reproduced by permission of the Kennel Club)

Not all dogs are officially recognized by the Kennel Club. These include:

Jack Russell Terriers. These dogs have been bred for their working abilities for many generations. Their appearance can vary, and this includes size, coat texture, shape and temperament.

Working sheepdogs. This term is used to describe the type of dog often seen working on farms and kept by many as pets. They are often referred to as "Border Collies." They are likely to have strong working instincts, and be energetic and active, requiring a great deal of exercise.

Lurchers. Originally, a greyhound/Border Collie mix. Traditionally bred by gypsies or poachers, with the aim of producing a dog with the speed of a greyhound and the trainability of a Border Collie to catch and retrieve rabbits. Nowadays, a lurcher is a type of dog, and may have many different breeds in his genetic makeup.

Gundog

Labrador Retriever · Cocker Spaniel · Golden Retriever · English Springer Spaniel · Weimaraner

Terrier

West Highland White · Staffordshire Bull Terrier · Border Terrier · English Bull Terrier

Utility

Lhasa Apso · Shih Tzu · Dalmatian · Miniature Schnauzer

Toy

Cavalier King Charles Spaniel · Yorkshire Terrier · Bichon Frise

Working

Boxer · Rottweiler · Dobermann

Pastoral

German Shepherd Dog

First cross. This is a dog whose parents were both pedigrees, with known parentage, but of different breeds.

Crossbreed. Technically, this is a dog with known parents, although each parent may contain a variety of breeds.

Mongrel. Technically, a mongrel is a dog of unknown parentage. Although this is often used as a derogatory term by many people and breeders, mongrels form a large part of the dog population and there are many wonderful, unique characters among them.

Our lives with dogs have changed dramatically over the generations. Selective breeding and changes in lifestyle have meant that there are many different types of dogs, and varying reasons for keeping them as pets. Even over the last 30 years, the dog's place in our family has altered beyond recognition. Dogs are now seen as closer members of the family, enjoying a position at the center of our lives. However, there is also a disadvantage. We expect so much of our dogs, often likening them to "little people," instead of understanding about their needs as a dog. Not surprisingly, this can lead to problems. This may be because owners and dogs have very different expectations of life together, or it may be because of the stress of family life, of which our dogs are more a part. Consequently, owning a dog can sometimes become more difficult and less enjoyable than was at first anticipated.

A generation ago, most dogs were not even allowed upstairs, let alone on the bed, but recent studies show that an increasing number of dogs today are allowed this privilege

Although many people feel they want their dog to be "just a pet," think of what this means. Very often, pet dogs have the most demands made upon them, and it is not surprising that some dogs are unable to cope with this.

Life Skills

Changes for the Dog

Recent advances in veterinary care enable many dogs to lead longer, healthier lives. Increased knowledge of pet nutrition means that dogs are able to be better fed than ever before. But on the negative side, there is an increased feeling against dogs in general. They are restricted and excluded more than they were before, and dogs today are expected to be far better behaved than ever in the past. Being a dog can be great, being a dog owner can be hard work!

Consider:

• We take it for granted that our dog likes to be with us, but we expect him to be happy to be left alone.

• When we do leave him, we give him access to our home and assume that he will not make any mistakes.

How does your dog feel when left alone?

• We expect him to get on with all other people and dogs that we meet and like ourselves.

• When visitors come, we want our dog to welcome them, yet we want him to deter intruders.

• If we bring other dogs, animals, or people into our family, we expect him to like them as much as we do.

• We let him off the leash, since we know he enjoys a run, but we expect him to come back to us when we call him.

• We select a dog bred for an activity, such as a Border Collie, for example, and then expect him to do nothing for a large proportion of the time.

• We expect him to understand what it is we want and give less thought to what he needs.

• We are allowed to have bad moods, maybe even taking this out on the dog, but he is never supposed to be grumpy.

• We give our dog all the privileges, but do not want him to take them for granted.

Many dogs accept and cope with all this and more and lead happy lives in a domestic situation. However, some dogs do have difficulties, and so we must take steps to reduce the likelihood of problems before they occur.

There is no other species of animal that we would take to the local park, let run free, and then expect to come back when we want them. However, this is what we expect our dogs to do for us.

a dog's eye view
senses

N.B. These games are not intended as tests of your dog's hearing, sight, etc. They are designed to help us understand our dogs a little better and appreciate their abilities. The results will depend on many factors, including your dog's relationship with you and how much practice he has had playing this type of game.

If you have any concerns about your dog's sensory abilities, speak to your veterinarian.

Smell

A dog's scenting ability is so much better than ours that it is hard for us to begin to understand what the world is like for our dog. It has been estimated that a dog's sense of smell is up to one million times greater than ours. Scent is usually the dog's dominant sense, whereas humans rely on sight above all else. One way to imagine the difference is to compare watching a hazy black-and-white, badly filmed programe on a television set with a small screen, compared to seeing the world normally, with perfect vision. The richness of a dog's world comes via his sense of smell.

Not only can he smell things, he also has an extra sense organ, called the Jacobson's organ. Since this is lacking in

For a dog, sniffing around is a natural behavior and a source of great stimulation and pleasure. It could be compared to reading a newspaper, watching the news, and listening to the neighbors all at once!

A cross-section of a dog's nose

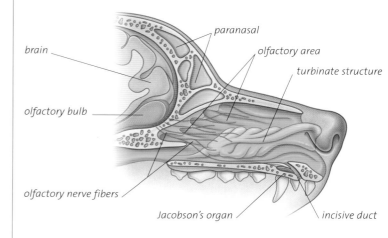

brain

paranasal

olfactory area

turbinate structure

olfactory bulb

olfactory nerve fibers

Jacobson's organ

incisive duct

Try This:

Use a tiny piece of a food that your dog likes. Strong smelling cheese, liver or chicken are usually good. Remove your dog from the room, so that he cannot see you. Place the food somewhere out of obvious sight, on the floor, for example just around the corner of a chair. Let your dog back in, and watch. Do not tell him to look for anything. Notice his reactions and how long it takes him to find the treat. Repeat in three different rooms.

If he finds the food in 0–5 seconds each time—he is obviously very tuned in to what is going on around him, and has a well-developed sense of smell.

5–20 seconds—he is good at using his sense of smell.

20 seconds–1 minute—he knows something is around and works well.

Up to 5 minutes, following lots of sniffing around—he's trying, admire his persistence and concentration.

More than 5 minutes or no attempt—are you sure your dog wanted the food?

Try some of the games in section 3 (pp. 116–119) to give him more practice.

humans, it is hard to describe its effect, but it is thought that it allows dogs to "taste" smells. The organ is situated on the roof of the dog's mouth, at the front. When a dog finds a particularly interesting scent, sometimes he will open his mouth while sniffing to allow this extra organ to work. Man has made use of this ability in everyday life. Dogs are trained to follow the scent of people, to detect substances such as drugs, to find delicacies such as truffles, and to differentiate between scents.

Because of their incredible ability to detect scents, we have trained dogs to help us. This includes locating people, tracking criminals, finding lost objects, and many other useful activities.

Sight

Generally speaking, sight is not the dominant sense in the dog. However, because it is *our* dominant sense, we often stimulate it and place more importance on it, resulting in our dogs becoming more reliant on it.

Some breeds have better eyesight than others. For example, Border Collies are known to be able to see well and are extremely responsive to movement. They are able to stare at something in order to react to any movement.

Dogs do not have the clarity of vision that we enjoy, but they can detect movement. Studies have shown that they cannot see colors with the richness we do, but it seems that they can differentiate colors, in the same way that we can when watching a black-and-white television set.

A cross-section of a dog's eye

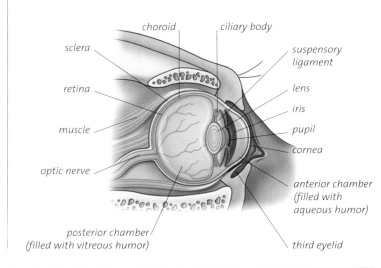

choroid • ciliary body • sclera • suspensory ligament • retina • lens • iris • muscle • pupil • cornea • optic nerve • anterior chamber (filled with aqueous humor) • posterior chamber (filled with vitreous humor) • third eyelid

Try This:

Throw a tasty treat or toy to your dog to catch. Repeat five times. How many does he catch?

CATCHES 5 OUT OF 5:
Well done, your dog can obviously see well and has good reactions. Some dogs can achieve this immediately, others need to practice first.

3 OR 4 OUT OF 5:
Well done, your dog obviously reacts well and is watching you.

2 OR 1 OUT OF 5:
Maybe your dog is less keen on this game or has had less practice.

0 OUT OF 5:
Either your dog is not interested in this game or does not know what it is that you want.

A cross-section of a dog's ear

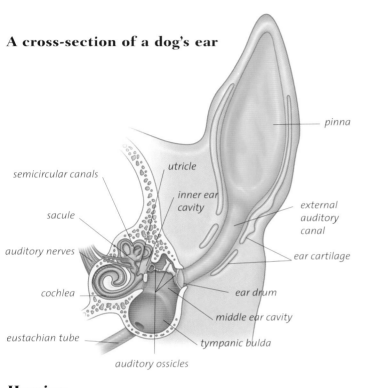

- pinna
- utricle
- semicircular canals
- inner ear cavity
- sacule
- external auditory canal
- auditory nerves
- ear cartilage
- cochlea
- ear drum
- middle ear cavity
- eustachian tube
- tympanic bulda
- auditory ossicles

Hearing

Dogs can hear a greater range of sounds than we can, but again, there are breed differences. Studies show that dogs can hear sounds much higher than the human ear can detect. They can also respond to lower tones. Many dogs show what owners lovingly refer to as "selective hearing." Their dog appears to be oblivious to being called or told what to do but responds instantly to his food bowl being moved. This has nothing to do with hearing abilities but everything to do with previous learning experiences.

It is amazing that dogs can filter out a great deal of noise and respond to something that is of interest to them. Many dogs hear the sound of their owner's car arriving home, yet ignore others. Because of their sensitive hearing, it is not surprising that many dogs suffer on hearing certain noises, especially fireworks. If we find them loud and startling, it must be frightening and possibly painful for some dogs.

Touch

Dogs vary considerably in their reaction to touch. Many breeds that were bred for being in contact with others have a relatively high tolerance to touch. An anxious dog is likely to be more reactive to being touched than a relaxed dog. A dog who has learned that being touched is pleasant is more likely enjoy it and tolerate it when it is necessary.

Try This:

How sensitive is your dog to touch?

Where does he best like or not like to be touched?

Is he happy for you to hold his feet?

If you touch him when he is not expecting it, does he flinch?

All of this is important when learning more about your dog. Did you know the answers to these questions or did you have to try them out?

If your dog is happy to be touched, he is less likely to react if you accidentally stand on his paw, and probably finds routine trips to the vet less stressful.

If your dog does not like being touched, either he has had some bad experiences or he is highly touch sensitive. He may find grooming unpleasant and may react more if you accidentally stand on him.

Taste

While some dogs will eat anything, others won't. Studies have shown that taste is the least important of the dog's senses. This explains why some dogs will often eat items that we consider unpleasant.

Sixth sense?

It has been suggested that dogs are able to sense things that we cannot. This has been attributed to a sixth sense. It is possible that they do possess some kind of sixth sense, but it cannot be proved. However, if we look at dogs' abilities, we can see that they are capable of things we are not. In many instances, this is because the dog's other senses are superior to ours, so it appears like a sixth sense.

Try This:

Offer your dog three different types of dog food.

Does he differentiate between the three? Does he eat everything, starting with the nearest? Does he differentiate but still eat everything in front of him?

This will tell you how important taste is to him.

Try This:

When your dog is not looking at you, simply think very hard about him looking at you. Do not move, just think about him. Do this for about 30 seconds. Does your dog turn to look at you? Repeat 5 times in the house and 5 times outside the house at different times of the day.

On a walk, try the same exercise. Does he turn to look at you?

If your dog doesn't look at you on any occasion: this is normal.

If he looks at you once or twice: some dogs will do this by chance, or it may be that he does know when you are thinking of him.

3–8: it would be unlikely that this was purely chance. Maybe your dog is extremely well tuned into you.

More than 8: it would be unlikely that this was chance. Perhaps you and your dog are extremely close. Make sure that you are not giving cues without meaning to, such as putting your hand in your pocket or making some sound.

Is your dog more aware of things than you realize? He may not have human abilities, but take time to understand and appreciate his canine attributes.

communication

Although dogs do not have the power of speech, they are experts at communication. Much of it is soundless. This does not mean that it is not occurring.

Smell

Dogs leave olfactory messages for each other all the time. They are less able to sweat through their skin as we can, but they do sweat through their paws. This means that each time a paw touches the ground, it leaves information for other dogs. Marking with urine or feces is another powerful communicator. Many owners of male dogs are amazed that their dogs can leave a few drops in important places. Lifting their leg is a way of raising the scent, making it even easier to notice. Some female dogs will also mark their territory in this way.

We are also unaware of the scents that we emit, such as when we are frightened, excited, or annoyed. We should not be surprised when our dog reacts to these.

Sound

Dogs do communicate by sound, but less so than by smell. Noises that dogs can make include:

Barking. This is the one we are most familiar with. It has many different uses and most owners can differentiate between different barks. Barking can be for a number of

---

Communication

The Importance of Smell

Sniffing is vital to a dog. It provides information about their world which we cannot even begin to comprehend. Even while walking along, a dog is taking in scents and learning about what is going on. Therefore, it is unfair to deny a dog these opportunities. Although a dog should not sniff every lamppost, he should know that there are times when he can spend as long as he wishes on a scent. Sniffing can be likened to reading the morning papers, or watching the news and discussing it with a friend.

reasons; for attention, to raise the alarm, as a demand, or as a show of aggression.

Growling. This is likely to be a warning that the dog is unhappy with the situation. Some dogs are more vocal than others and will growl more readily.

Howling. Some dogs howl more than others. In wolves, howling is a social activity as well as a way of keeping in contact. Some dogs howl in response to certain tones they hear, perhaps on TV or from a musical instrument. Others howl when they are feeling lonely, whereas some dogs will never howl.

Whining. This is a noise heard frequently in puppies. It tends to means that they are unhappy with something and it is a cry for help. Many dogs learn that it brings them what they want, and so it continues into adulthood.

Yelping. This is normally a quick cry of pain. It is probably subconscious, rather than communication.

Touch

Touch is used less often, but dogs are similar to humans in that they can use it as an aggressive signal, for example pushing another out of the way, or it can be a demonstration of affection, such as curling up and touching another to sleep.

Taste

It seems unlikely that taste is used in communication except in conjunction with smell, and when the dog is using the Jacobson's organ.

A bark can mean anything from "Hello" to "Go away."

Touching can be something that is enjoyable for dog and owner, but it can communicate other feelings in different circumstances.

body language

When looking at body language, it is important to understand that similar signals can have different meanings, even when used by the same dog.

Breed and individual differences

Be aware of what is normal for a breed or individual dog. For example:

• A terrier is likely to carry his tail high when relaxed, whereas most whippets will have a lower tail carriage.
• A cocker spaniel cannot signal with his ears as a German Shepherd can.
• An individual dog may have a tendency to put his hackles up as soon as he is aroused. This may be because of excitement or aggression.

Look at your dog

Watch your own dog and dogs in general and learn from them. They can teach you more than any book.

Overall picture

Always look at the overall picture, rather than concentrating on one aspect. Compare human behavior—a smile can mean friendliness or anticipation, embarrassment or lack of interest. Therefore, it is important to see the whole picture in context.

Body shape

• As a general rule, a relaxed dog will look like one.
• A dog who is threatening or intimidating will attempt to look larger. He will stand more upright, with his head and tail up. Hackles may be raised.
• A frightened dog will attempt to look smaller, by cowering, head and tail down, and crouching.

Ears

• A relaxed dog will have his ears in a neutral position. This will vary for different breeds.
• An alert dog will prick his ears or move them forward, in order to detect every sound.
• A frightened dog will put his ears back.
• A very unhappy dog will pin his ears back so that they are flat to his head.

Eyes

Eye contact is extremely important. It can be friendly or unfriendly, a challenge or a sign of aggression, or a loving way of communicating.
• A frightened dog may feel the need to stare at the object of his fear, whereas a submissive dog is likely to look away.
• A dog who is challenging will probably stare directly. An apprehensive dog may give a glare, followed by a growl if the threat continues.
• A happy, relaxed dog will stare in a friendly way.
• A dog who is attempting to get attention from people can stare for a considerable time until they take notice of him. Direct eye contact tends to show that the dog is concentrating on a particular object, person or dog.

Lips and mouth

• Again, a happy dog will be relaxed around his mouth.
• A tense dog will tense his lips.
• After a growl, many dogs will pull back their lips in a snarl, showing their teeth.

The tail can be likened to a flag—a dog is able to see the outline from a distance and be immediately

aware of the intentions of the other dog. However, when we interfere by removing part or all of the tail, we

are removing this extremely valuable method of canine communication.

Tail

The tail is extremely important to a dog and also for the owner, since it is an excellent indicator of what kind of mood the dog is in and how he needs to be treated.

As a rough guide, the higher the tail is, the more aroused a dog is. A relaxed dog will hold his tail in a neutral position, and an anxious dog will lower his tail, often putting it between his legs if he is really unhappy. A wagging tail is not always an indication of friendliness. It is safer to read it as a sign of anticipation. Therefore, a dog wagging his tail may be friendly, but he may also be looking towards a confrontation or show of aggression. A relaxed dog will move his tail in a relaxed way. A dog who is tense and alert will wag his tail more stiffly. An excited dog will wag his tail quickly, often moving the whole of his back end if he is really pleased to see you!

Communication

Hackles

These are the hairs along the line of the dog's back. Most often, they will only raise them around the shoulder area, but when very aroused, they can often raise a ridge along the length of their spine. Again, it is an attempt to look larger and more threatening. Some dogs will raise their hackles very readily, which may be a sign of arousal rather than aggression.

Other signals

Dogs use many other signals. For example:

A *yawn* can be a sign of stress or an attempt to defuse a difficult situation.

Sniffing the ground can be a displacement activity, when the dog is unsure what to do next.

The *"play bow"* is often seen in puppies and young dogs when they are expecting a game. This is when the front end of the dog is lowered and the back end is up, tail wagging. It is also seen in dogs who are unsure about the reaction they will receive.

Dogs communicate well and they usually understand one another. However, we intervene and this can cause problems. Dogs in today's society must wear a leash at all times, but this restricts their natural behavior and communication. Although it cannot be avoided, it helps to be aware of this.

Lying down when approaching another dog can show that he is unsure of the situation or that he wants to chase.

Jumping up can have different meanings. It can be a submissive gesture, a demanding action or a learned reaction. It is generally not desirable behavior.

The function of body language

The whole aim of body language and communication is to promote peaceful living and avoid aggression. Even the most aggressive looking dog, snarling and growling, is trying to avoid physical aggression. He will use it but only as a very last resort.

Reading our body language

Most pet dogs are wonderful at reading our body language, even though it is different from their own. They know immediately when we are happy, sad, cross, excited, and so

When reading body language, look at the dog as a whole, rather than looking at certain parts only, or simply judging on the basis of the breed alone.

A smile means friendliness and a hand shake is a greeting, but there is more to it than this. For example, a person can smile with their mouth, but their eyes can convey a different meaning.

on. Many owners report that they only need to think about taking their dog for a walk for him to respond immediately. They are just as quick to learn the signals for less pleasant things, such as when we are going to leave them.

When training, many dogs find it easier to respond to hand signals and body language than to listen to the words we use. Are we more consistent with these? Or are they easier for a dog to learn?

Dogs spend a great deal of their time watching us. They learn to respond to us and understand what we do. Maybe this is easier for our dogs. After all, they do not have as many things in life to think about as we do. But surely, when we are supposedly the more intelligent half of the partnership that exists between us, it is important for us to learn just as much from them.

Instead of always trying to tell our dogs what to do, we should simply watch them more and learn from them. Instead of talking, we should listen. Instead of demanding, we should watch. This way, we can begin to let our dogs teach us how to understand them.

establishing
good behavior

2

It is now known that a great deal of learning occurs when the puppy is very young. The period from a few weeks old to five months is extremely important. This is when puppies learn much of what will influence their adult behavior. The foundations laid now will affect his behavior for the rest of his life. Therefore, the sooner we start teaching our young puppies, showing them how we would like them to behave and rewarding them for good behavior, the better life will be for everyone.

Dogs learn throughout their lives and the points outlined in this chapter apply to all dogs. While it is true that young dogs do learn more quickly than older dogs, you can teach an old dog new tricks. So when is the best age to start teaching our dog? The age he is now!

socialization

What do we want of our puppy as he grows up? Just to be well behaved, happy and confident. Just! We ask so much of our pet dogs, but we can help them greatly by introducing them to situations in the right way and helping them to like people when they are young.

The first few months of his life is when your puppy learns the most. He will continue to learn throughout his life, but the rate of learning will slow down. Therefore, we must make the most of these early days to give our puppy a good foundation. Don't worry if your dog or puppy is already past this stage.

A puppy learns extremely quickly—make sure he is learning the behavior you want.

Socialization becomes harder but is still possible. Read the advice here and apply it to your own dog. If you have a dog who is older than four months, who shows no problem behavior, a similar process should be followed.

Socialization involves the puppy having good experiences in lots of situations, but be careful not to overwhelm him.

However, if your dog is already showing any undesirable habits, you must take things more gradually. For more details on curing unwanted habits, see chapter 4.

What is socializing?

Socializing is not simply letting your puppy grow up, hoping he will learn what you want. It is an active process of teaching your puppy how to cope and behave in different situations, through good experiences. It will vary according to your puppy's age and temperament. A shy and timid puppy needs to learn to enjoy the company of other people, whereas a confident and exuberant youngster needs to learn manners, how to greet people without jumping up, and how to listen to his owner despite distractions. Socializing should continue through your dog's life, to give him the opportunity to continue practicing his social skills.

Safe socializing

As well as insuring your puppy's mental development, you need to consider his physical well-being. Young puppies should complete their vaccination program before being exposed to sources of infectious diseases. Talk to your own veterinarian, ideally before you acquire your puppy, so that you know when to take him along for his first series of vaccinations.

Your puppy should begin going out and about with you as soon as it is safe to do so.

You must protect your puppy from coming into contact with these potentially fatal diseases. For some time, the advice was simply to keep him indoors, away from everyone. However, this also meant denying him vital learning experiences during this critical stage.

A program of "safe socializing" is the best option. This involves giving our puppy the maximum pleasant learning experiences, with the least possible risk to his health.

It can include:

- Carrying your puppy out and about
- Short car journeys
- Inviting friends to your home to meet and play with your puppy
- Visiting friends' homes, preferably with an enclosed back yard, so that your puppy begins to explore
- Meeting friendly dogs—as long as the other dog is healthy and fully vaccinated, the risks are minimal while the gains are immense. Take care, use common sense.

Take extra care if you live in, or are visiting, an area where infectious diseases are known to abound.

An increasing number of veterinarians are now holding Puppy Parties. These are an excellent way of introducing your puppy to many wonderful experiences and getting him to meet other puppies and their owners. Ask at your own practice for advice and details.

Socializing

The following principles apply at all times:

• Your puppy needs a wide range of experiences.

• Your puppy needs frequent experiences.

• Experiences must be pleasant. Your puppy must enjoy meeting people, not simply tolerate them.

• Your puppy must learn the right behaviors.

• If your puppy shows any signs of apprehension, do not rush to comfort him. Your attention is seen as a reward and will make him more likely to show these signs again. Simply show him that you are confident, by ignoring what is happening. Take things more gradually in the future.

• If your puppy shows signs of nervousness, you are trying to progress too quickly. Simply remove him from the situation, without undue attention from you, and progress more slowly and tactfully.

• Do not let your puppy become overexcited. As with the nervous puppy, take things more slowly and remember to reward good, calm behavior.

Life Skills

Habituation

Habituation involves helping a puppy to become accustomed to the sights, sounds and scents of our world, by introducing him in a controlled way. It involves walking him past roadworks, helping him to learn not to be afraid of traffic, people with baby carriages, etc. Take him out and about, progressing at his own rate, so that he learns to take all new experiences that he encounters in his stride.

Meeting people

Whatever kind of life you lead, your puppy needs to learn how to relate to and behave with other people. Most puppies become slightly more introverted as they grow older. Therefore, learning to enjoy being with other people is vital. Puppies need good experiences with a wide variety of people. Make sure that your puppy meets and enjoys old and young people, men and women, people with hats, sunglasses, beards, wheelchairs, etc. Whatever he learns

1. Aim to encounter lots of different situations while you walk with your puppy or dog.

2. Either arrange to meet people or make the most of each situation you come across.

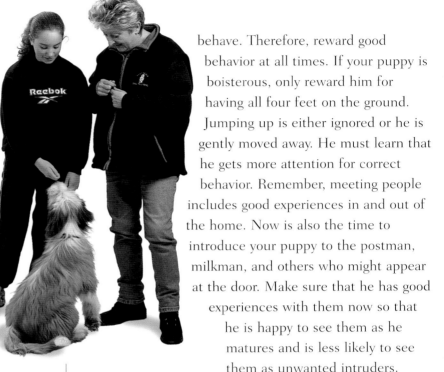

now, he will accept as normal as he grows up. The first time he meets a police officer, for example, he may well think she looks strange as he has never before met anyone dressed in uniform, carrying a gun and stick. If he enjoys being around her, because she makes a fuss of him and gives him some treats, he will learn that even people who look different are good fun to be with. The more good experiences he has, the more he will be able to cope with other situations that he comes across.

You must also teach manners, since you do not want your adolescent dog to learn that rushing up to everyone and jumping around is an acceptable way to behave. Therefore, reward good behavior at all times. If your puppy is boisterous, only reward him for having all four feet on the ground. Jumping up is either ignored or he is gently moved away. He must learn that he gets more attention for correct behavior. Remember, meeting people includes good experiences in and out of the home. Now is also the time to introduce your puppy to the postman, milkman, and others who might appear at the door. Make sure that he has good experiences with them now so that he is happy to see them as he matures and is less likely to see them as unwanted intruders.

Above: Although it may seem appealing when he is a young, cute puppy, remember that your puppy will grow and therefore it is important that he is rewarded for the right behavior from the beginning.

3. Make sure that your dog is rewarded for doing what you have asked him to do.

4. Rewards should come from the other people involved, if possible, or from you.

meeting **children**

Although we know that children are the same species as "people," we could forgive our dog for not understanding this, if we have not taught him from an early age. It is vital that he has good experiences with children of all ages. Babies make strange noises and move in odd ways. Toddlers jump and scream. Older children shout and slam doors. All of these behaviors can be extremely unnerving for a dog who is only used to calm, predictable adults. Therefore, set up situations where children meet with your dog, in the home and outside, and make sure that all experiences are good. Always keep a very close eye on any interaction between children and dogs. Both can behave very unpredictably. Children and dogs have different ideas about what constitutes a game, and things can quickly get out of hand. Again, reward good behavior and insist that ground rules are followed.

If you are using treats, make sure that the dog does not snatch or jump and that the child does not tease.

If you are using a toy, the games should not become rough or out of control. Calm games of hiding the toy are better than games involving everyone running around.

If the child is stroking the dog, make sure that the child is gentle and that the dog is finding this to be a pleasant and enjoyable experience.

Going for walks together is often a good idea since the children and dog can enjoy each other's company but still have other things to engage their interest.

Puppies and children should always be supervised, to insure that both are learning how to understand the other. Encourage calm games and affection. As your puppy learns to respond to you, encourage children to follow your example, always under close supervision, so that you can intervene if either begins to be too rough.

Meeting other dogs

Your puppy needs to have a wide range of experiences with different types of dogs. The encounters must be pleasant for your puppy, in order for him to gain confidence, so you need to select your puppy's "friends" carefully. Initially, calm, friendly dogs are the best since they will not become overboisterous. When your puppy is confident, progress to a wider range. Ideally, your dog needs to meet good natured dogs of all shapes and sizes.

Do not be too overprotective. As your puppy learns more about dogs, it is good for him to learn that some dogs will ignore him, and some will even tell him to stop with a glare or low growl. As long as the dog is good tempered, he will not hurt your puppy but will be teaching him an important lesson in dog manners.

Meeting other animals

It is a good idea to take your puppy to places where he will be around other animals, not just puppies and dogs. Here, you expect different things from him. You do not want your puppy to approach a horse to make friends or play, for example. He needs to know that they exist but that you are more important. Keep at a distance where your puppy is not overexcited and can still listen to you. Read the following section about being the most important part of your dog's life.

your puppy and **you**

You must be the most important thing to your puppy at all times. Although socializing is vital for a puppy to develop into a well-adjusted adult, you also need a dog who is under your control, and so you need your puppy to know that at all times, you, the owner, are the most important and interesting thing in his life, even when other things are going on.

Therefore, view this as a seesaw, with social behavior on one end and your dog's relationship with you on the other. If you have an extrovert puppy who loves the world, it is likely that he sometimes forgets about you, and this can lead to a lack of control. You need to spend time reminding him that although other people and dogs are great fun to be with, you are even better!

This means playing games, rewarding good behavior and generally controlling the situation so that your puppy does not forget about you. Do not scold him and become angry, since this will convince him that other people, dogs or scents on the ground are much more fun to be around.

Your puppy should enjoy being with you and want to be involved. If he would rather be somewhere else, training, walking and playing will all be more difficult.

On the other hand, if you have a more sensitive and timid puppy, he already knows that you are the center of his universe. However, you may have more difficulty in persuading him to enjoy the company of others in the same way. Therefore, you will have to make sure that he has some pleasant experiences with other people for him to boost his confidence and make him more sociable.

Balancing this seesaw is important and must continue throughout your dog's life.

Example 1. As your cute puppy grows into a gangly adolescent, it is normal for him to test the boundaries and develop his independence by wandering further afield and becoming less responsive. Do not become cross and annoyed. Remember the seesaw. All this will do is confirm in his mind that everyone else is more interesting, and he will be even less responsive. Therefore, be consistent and become more interesting. Play lots of games and have fun training sessions while continuing your socializing to make sure that your dog enjoys being with others, but is in no doubt that you are the most exciting person to be with.

Example 2. The summer time is great for being out and about, having fun. Socialization becomes easier, since there are people, children, and dogs everywhere. Playing games and being involved with your dog is also easier, since the weather makes it less of a chore to be outdoors with him. However, as the days become colder, wetter, and darker, walking the dog is less inviting, and on the walks you take, you will meet fewer people. Therefore, at this time it is essential to remember the seesaw and set up situations where you will have the opportunity to socialize your dog.

Puppies tend to have an extremely short attention span and can easily be distracted. Do not expect him to concentrate for too long—keep sessions short and fun.

puppy problem solver
encouraging good behavior

Many people fail to realize that however sweet puppies are, they learn very quickly. Behavior they find rewarding when they are small will be continued as they grow into adolescents and adult dogs.

So how do you teach your puppy what it is that you want?

1. Do not be cross

Your puppy has no idea what is expected of him, so it is up to you to teach him. Do not become angry when he makes a mistake, just use it as an opportunity to teach him what is right. Avoid punishment. How can he know what you want when you have not taught him?

2. Reward good behavior

Puppies learn very quickly through reward. If a puppy does something and something pleasant follows, he is more likely to repeat this action. Almost all training is based on this simple rule. Therefore, notice when your puppy does the right thing and reward him in an appropriate way.

3. Ignore unwanted behavior

It is tempting to shout at your puppy when he makes a mistake. However, this can simply make matters worse. Instead, ignore minor misdemeanors.

4. Interrupt behavior that cannot be ignored

In order for your puppy to learn, you must teach him. If he is chewing the chair leg, say "no" and gently move him. Give him one of his own toys to chew and reward him for paying attention to it. If your puppy is sniffing the ground and seems about to empty himself, distract him, and take him outside. Wait with him and reward him for emptying himself there.

5. Accept that he will not get things right all the time

Your puppy will make mistakes—this is normal. Do not expect too much too soon. For example, mouthing should decrease, but it will be a few weeks before it stops altogether.

6. Your puppy will learn what you teach him

If your puppy continues to make mistakes, he is not being naughty or difficult. He is probably just confused and this is due to your teaching. If your puppy is not learning the right behaviors, it is not his fault. You should change your approach.

Ouch! The only way a puppy can learn what is expected of him is when we teach him.

7. If you teach him what is wrong, you must teach him what is right

It is easy to say "no," but this does not teach a puppy what you want. Interrupt unwanted behavior but always show your puppy what it is you want and reward him for this.

8. Be consistent

It is no good if you let your puppy jump up one day, because you are wearing old clothes, but get cross with him the next because you are dressed to go to work. Your puppy does not understand the difference. He will simply become confused and will not obey you.

Also, all members of the family must agree to enforce the same rules. There may be a rule that the puppy is not fed from the table, but if the children find it funny to feed him their unwanted scraps, or your husband likes to share his toast with the puppy, he will become confused as to what is acceptable behavior and what is not.

A good relationship between owner and dog is at the center of all teaching and learning.

setting ground rules

The Smith family were delighted with their new puppy, Max. He was so funny when he jumped up, looked cute when he chewed on their fingers, and the children thought it was a great game when he ran off with their toys and they had to chase him around the house to wrestle with him to retrieve them. "He's a real character," laughed Mrs. Smith to her friends. But a few months later, there was less to laugh about. The children could not bring their friends home because Max knocked them over in his greeting. Max would mouth and chew on hands, arms, and legs, which was beginning to be less than pleasant. But

---

Life Skills

Many people are concerned by the "mad five minutes" that most puppies have. This is where the puppy puts his ears back and tail down and hurtles around at great speed. Some dogs continue this into adulthood, but it will decrease or stop. There are various reasons:
1. Normal puppy behavior
2. A release of energy
3. Pure pleasure, attention or to relieve stress
The best thing to do is to ignore the behavior as much as possible. Leave the room, remove valuable objects, and encourage the puppy into another area, such as the yard, if necessary.

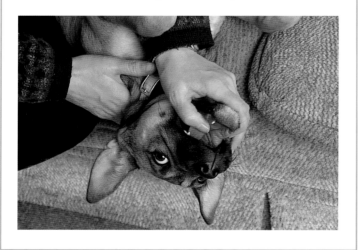

Remember, small puppies grow into bigger dogs. Behaviors which your puppy learns at this age will stay with him throughout his life. Make sure that he learns what you want.

when Max snapped at Katie when she was struggling to remove her doll from his mouth, the Smith family were forced to realize that this cute puppy was behaving in a way that was unacceptable. "But he used to be so good and funny," said Mrs. Smith. "What went wrong?"

Max, as we can see, was simply continuing the behaviors that he had learned as a young puppy. The habits had been encouraged. How was Max to understand that someone had changed the rules?

Always bear this in mind. A puppy is fun to have on your knee and to roll around with on the bed, but will you want him to do this when he is fully grown? When your puppy is bigger, will you want him jumping on the furniture or on the bed? Bear in mind that there will be times when he is muddy. You may have visitors who do not want him on their knee. Jumping up may seem cute at the moment, but this habit is extremely persistent. It is better to teach your puppy now that he only gets attention for having all four feet on the floor.

The habits that you encourage now will be much harder to break in the future. It is far easier for you and your dog to learn the rules now.

The same is true of all dogs, especially rescue and re-homed dogs who may be older when they arrive into your household. They still learn quickly and so it is always best to consider and set the ground rules at the beginning when your dog is young, and then stick to them.

As discussed later, rules can be relaxed as time goes by and your dog earns extra privileges but, at first, stick to the ground rules that you feel happy with.

Teach by rewarding good behavior rather than being cross with unwanted behavior. Make sure that your dog learns that it is more rewarding to be on the ground, since this is where he gets lots of attention. All good things stop if he jumps up.

mouthing
people and clothing

Before Pete and Denise acquired their new puppy, Denise read all the books and felt she had a good idea of what to expect. Therefore, she was not surprised when Sophie started mouthing. She followed all the advice to the letter but was surprised and concerned when Sophie's mouthing became harder and she would snap and growl when doing it. Pete was also surprised. However, on watching Pete and Sophie together, Denise noticed that Pete was doing the opposite of many of the things she believed in. He was playing lots of rough and tumble games. Consequently, Sophie became overexcited and boisterous and would then begin biting hard, whereupon Pete would shout and whack her on the nose, and Sophie would go and lie down in a

An action which may have been amusing in a puppy is not so cute when he is a fully grown dog.

corner. Denise explained why she felt this was not good for Sophie and asked Pete to read the books. Pete agreed to stop rough games and play games with toys instead, and within two weeks, Sophie's behavior was much calmer.

Mouthing and play biting are to be expected in a young puppy, but it is essential that he learns that it is not

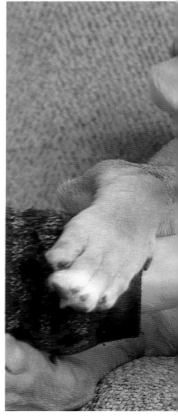

acceptable to put his teeth on to people. A puppy has extremely sharp teeth. When he is young, he explores everything by testing it with his mouth. In the litter, he would have played with his siblings and should have learned that if he mouthed too hard, it hurt his playmate, who would probably yelp and then refuse to play.

When he comes to live with a family of humans, the puppy needs to learn that humans are even more fragile than puppies and that if he even thinks about putting his teeth on us, it hurts and all good things stop. This is how he learns "bite inhibition." A dog who does not learn this can be dangerous, since if he chooses to bite, he has no idea how to inhibit the pressure.

Therefore:
- **Do** expect your puppy to mouth.
- **Do not** become cross with him.
- **Do not** hit him, especially on the nose.
- **Don't** waggle your finger in front of his mouth.
- **Do** give him alternative things to chew and reward him for this behavior.
- **Do** avoid rough games that encourage mouthing.
- **Do** play games where the puppy puts a toy in his mouth.
- **When he mouths,** say "ow" and then reward him for stopping and give him something else to do.
- **If this does not work,** try a different noise, such as "ah," and then ignore him for a few moments.
- **Take extra care** if children are around, as puppies find children so interesting.
- **Resist the urge** to jump, run, or flap your hands about since this makes you more interesting to chew on.
- **Everyone in the family** must be consistent.
- **Do not** expect it to stop immediately, but the frequency and intensity should gradually reduce over the weeks.

Right: It is normal for a young puppy to mouth, but it is important that he learns that this is not an acceptable way to behave.

Left: Provide an alternative for the young puppy to chew, or distract him with something better. Scolding him or becoming cross could make the situation worse.

house **breaking**

One of the reasons that dogs are so successful as pets is that they can be taught to be clean in the house. House-breaking is usually the first thing you will teach your puppy, so not only do you want to get it right for the sake of your home, but also your puppy will be learning about you. If he learns that you are clear, consistent, and easy to understand, it is a good basis for everything else he needs to know. However, if he finds that you are unpredictable, inconsistent, and frightening, learning will be more difficult in the future.

Case Study

Digby

Fiona works for a local rescue center and she frequently fosters young dogs. Digby was sixteen weeks when his owners brought him to her. "He's such a dirty dog," they complained, "always messing in the bedrooms." Poor Digby had learned that everywhere was wrong to relieve himself and in an attempt to please his owners, he hid himself away when he needed to go. After three weeks of patience and conscientious watching, Digby had learned that outside was the place and soon, Digby went to a loving new home where his training was continued.

Puppies have an inbuilt need to keep their den clean. Even when tiny, they will try to go away from the nest to relieve themselves.

Your puppy will need to empty himself regularly. Take him out:

- on waking
- after playing
- after feeding or drinking
- after any excitement
- when he is awake and has not been out for an hour or so
- when he seems suddenly distracted, sniffing the ground, walking quickly in circles
- and many other times in between.

Do not simply let your puppy go into the yard since he may forget what he wanted. Go with him. When he empties himself, make a big fuss of him and give him a treat. This must happen immediately after he has finished. If you wait until you come back into the house, it is too late for him to make the connection.

If he does not empty himself, wait for about five minutes. (Time yourself—five minutes is an incredibly long time.) Do not distract him but encourage him to sniff around his favorite area. If he has not emptied himself, bring him back inside, but keep a close eye on him. He will need to go soon and you will need to recognize the signs so that he does not make a mistake.

Every mistake teaches your puppy the wrong habit. Every time he gets it right, he is learning the right behavior.

Although housebreaking can seem extremely time consuming in the early weeks, it is time well spent since you will have a dog who is reliably clean for many years to come.

Spanking him and "rubbing his nose in it" will only teach him that you are unpleasant and do strange, aggressive things to him. Success depends on your dedication and you need to be there, keeping an eye on your puppy. When you are not there, he cannot learn what you want. If you have to leave your puppy, restrict the area and put newspaper down. On your return, simply greet your puppy, clean the area, and remove the newspaper. If he has made a mistake, it is not his fault.

chewing

All puppies chew. We cannot and should not stop it. The trick is to direct the chewing on to the right objects, distracting him from chewing others. What does your puppy want to chew? Young puppies often prefer soft objects, whereas older puppies generally prefer hard objects. Most puppies like things that have "give" in them. This is why they may not be interested in "indestructible" toys and prefer flimsy items that they can destroy. All chews and toys you give your puppy must be safe to put in his mouth.

Puppies also love attention. If the puppy settles down to chew his toy, the owner ignores him. However, if he picks up the television remote control, they shout, they chase him, and he becomes the center of attention and has a great game. If you were a puppy, which would you choose to chew on?

Therefore, reward good behavior. When you see your puppy chewing the right object, go to him and give him some attention. Have interesting chews around and occasionally give him one and fuss over him as he is chewing it.

At first, keep interesting but forbidden items out of your puppy's reach. Children's toys, cigarette lighters, pens, paper, and clothing are all fascinating for puppies and easy for them to pick up.

When you make a mistake and your puppy gets something he should not have, do not overreact. If it is nothing important, it is a good idea to ignore your puppy, keeping an eye on him. We do not want him to think that grabbing objects results in your attention.

If it is something you cannot leave with your puppy, quietly go to him and remove it from him. There is no point in telling him to "drop" if he does not know this word. Do not be angry. Gently take it from him and praise him for giving it to you. Put the object away. If your puppy

---

Case Study

Tess

Tess, a ten-week-old puppy, found a box of tissues. What a great game she had! She pounced, chewed, and shredded. Soon she was tired and went for a sleep. Ten minutes later, Mrs. Jones realized she had not seen Tess for a while and went to look for her. She was relieved to find her asleep but not so impressed with the snowstorm that greeted her in the living room. She resolved to keep a closer eye on Tess, kept tissues out of the way, and felt grateful that Tess had not found anything more valuable or dangerous.

Dogs need to chew, especially when young. Provide safe, fun items to play with and to chew and encourage your dog to use them. If your dog is chewing a toy, he isn't destroying something more valuable.

There are huge selections of toys and chews available. Ask at your pet store and remember that a toy suitable for a small puppy is not necessarily still safe when he is fully grown.

Chewing is of great benefit to a dog. It is one of the most natural behaviors, but make sure that anything you give to him is safe and suitable for his age and size.

Find out your own dog's preference. Many young puppies prefer soft toys, whereas they tend to choose harder toys when they start teething. Some dogs prefer to play with toys as part of a game with you. Dogs who enjoy their food may like a toy stuffed with titbits.

needs to chew, give him an alternative toy or chewstick. If he wants something to occupy himself with, distract him and do something else more interesting with him. If your puppy begins to chew larger objects, such as furniture, say "no" and distract him. If problems persist or if your puppy is well-behaved when you are with him, but destroys items when he is left, this is a different problem. (Read chapter 4, pp. 134–135.)

pack **behavior**

Although we associate closely with our dogs and see them as one of the family, they are not simply little humans. We must understand the differences and expect our dogs to behave like dogs. Dogs are pack animals. A pack is a social group similar to a family, but because dogs cannot communicate through speech, the rules are more clearly defined and are followed strictly by all the members.

Before you acquire your new puppy, he will have had a six- to eight-week intensive course in dog behavior. Through his experiences with his litter mates and his mother, he already understands dog behavior but knows little of humans. In order for his puppy brain to make sense of his new life, he will assume that, although people look different, they must work to the same rules that he understands.

Every pack must have a clear, undisputed pack leader. Good pack leaders are not aggressive, they simply assume rights and responsibilities with their role.

Among his rights are:

Eating

The pack leader has the right to eat first and can often take food from others. When our puppy or dog comes to our home, we need to feed ourselves before we feed him, so he clearly understands that he is not the most important. Furthermore, we should not share our food with him, or he will get the idea that we will give up our food for him, because he is special.

Who is training whom?

Case Study

Rex

Rex picks up a toy and takes it to his owner, Jayne. Depending on the game he wants, he will either drop it at Jayne's feet, in which case, being a well-trained owner, she will pick it up and throw it absentmindedly as she watches television. Or Rex will push it into her hand. As soon as her hand closes over it, he will pull frantically. Or he will dance around in front of her, inviting her to try to grab it, which of course, Jayne does. The game continues for as long as Rex wants. Eventually he will take the toy, wander off, drop it, and settle down. Jayne is pleased that Rex has enjoyed his game, but what has he really learned? He has learned that he is totally in control of that game, which is probably repeated several times during the day, leaving him in no doubt that he is the best.

Games are not "just for fun." In your dog's mind, they are an important way of determining the hierarchy, testing boundaries, and learning consequences. Playing games is important, but you must understand the games your dog plays with you. Tug of war is not the best game for many dogs, but if you do choose to play it, will your dog let go of the toy when you ask him? It is important that you can control the game.

Playing games

Games are an important way of finding out who is the strongest, cleverest, most agile member of the pack. Unfortunately, our dog generally puts much more effort into these games than the humans do, and so often sees himself as the winner.

Sleeping

The top dog has the right to the best place to sleep. Generally, others will move out of his way, and not attempt to move him. It is rather like the boss's car parking space in the company car lot.

With our new dog, we often give him a bed which we are unlikely to go in. However, we may allow him on the furniture and all over the house, again showing him that he is the most important member of the family.

Do you allow your dog to sleep on your bed? Or does he allow you to sleep on his?

getting attention
and being touched

In a dog or wolf pack, the top dog decides who gives attention to whom, and for how long. He can invite others to touch him and will tell them when to stop. He can give attention to any of the others when he chooses.

Imagine how our new dog feels when he realizes that he can usually get attention any time from you, simply by looking cute. If that doesn't work, he can usually do something else, like barking or chewing the furniture, and someone will take notice of him. Attention is often so easy to get, that he feels he must be really special. On the other hand, sometimes he does not like the attention. Perhaps his owner is grooming him, and he is not so keen. He wriggles and struggles and maybe rolls around and mouths and eventually, if he tries hard enough, it will stop. So he learns something else. Unwanted attention can be stopped if you fight hard enough.

Rights of passage

The pack leader can go anywhere he chooses. No one will stop him or get in his way. In our heated homes, doors are rarely shut and our dogs

A dog who lies in the doorway or who pushes past you could be telling you that he is in charge.

have plenty of freedom. In addition, if our dog is lying in a doorway, we are unlikely to move him, preferring to step over him. He, on the other hand, has no hesitation about barging past his owners, whenever he chooses. If a door is shut, he can bark, whine, or scratch and usually it will be opened for him in the end.

We can see that, from our dog's point of view, he is now convinced that nice though his owners are, he is superior to them in every way. Not every dog will take advantage of this. Some dogs are happy to be looked after and will cause none of the above problems.

However, other dogs are more ambitious and feel that it is their right and duty to look after everyone lower down the pack and maintain pack cohesion. This is when problems can occur. Your dog may be less responsive than you would like and he may begin to show some signs of aggression to family members. He may object to visitors leaving the house, or develop any one of a range of serious or not-so-serious traits. Some owners are happy to live with this, but it is likely that this dog is not happy. He is confused. Why do his owners treat him like the most important member of the family most of the time, but expect him to be groomed, or do as he is told at others? This does not make any sense to his canine brain.

Some dogs are less assuming, but they instinctively know that their owner is not in charge. This can make them more anxious, since they feel they cannot trust their owner to look after them.

Daily grooming and handling is not just important for your dog's health and coat care, it is an important way of gently communicating that we have the right to do this. Grooming should be gentle and pleasant for the dog but must be on your terms.

By seeing the situation from our dog's point of view, we can see what changes we can make to the way we treat them. We simply need to use the same rules to promote ourselves and all members of the household.

By eating before your dog feeds and not sharing your food, your dog will learn that pestering is not rewarded and sooner or later will accept that his food comes later.

The following are good guidelines to implement, especially with young or opportunistic dogs. However, if you have an older dog and have no problems at all, do not feel you need to change things, just be aware at all times of how he perceives the situation.

Eating Feed your dog after you have eaten and do not share your food with him. Lots of treats should be given as rewards for good behavior, but they should always be earned and be separate from your food.

Sleeping Let your dog have his own resting areas, for example a basket, but make sure that you can call him away from it, to you, at times. Occasionally walk through his bed or rearrange the bedding, when he is not in it. Have your own exclusive areas where you can go, such as your bedroom, where your dog is not allowed.

Games You must be able to control the games (see pp. 120–121). Games should be fun, but make sure your dog is receiving the right messages.

Attention Your attention should come when you decide. Sometimes, ignore your dog when he pesters for attention. Ignoring means do not look at, speak to, or touch your dog.

It is important for a dog to have somewhere he can rest undisturbed, but also that he does not object if you stroke him when he is there.

Therefore, saying "go away" is not ignoring him, since he is still getting attention. At other times, call him to you for a fuss, and stop when you decide, not when he decides to wander away. Read the section on handling (pp. 64–65). Reward good behavior (see pp. 126–127).

Access Do not always allow your dog everywhere in the house. It is a good idea if he accepts that doors are closed from time to time. If he is lying in the doorway, call him away and reward him. (Do not do this if your dog is elderly, unwell or extremely tired.) Make sure that he can "wait" when you open doors if you ask him (see chapter 3). Do not allow him to barge past you. These rules should be followed to the same extent by everyone in the family. If there are any problems, read chapter 4.

Being a good pack leader also requires other attributes:
• Consistency is essential. You cannot change the rules to suit yourself, they must remain the same.
• Predictability is also needed. Your dog needs to know that you will not suddenly react in strange and scary ways.
• Patience and understanding are crucial: punishment will not help. Use of aggression will only teach your dog that whoever is the most aggressive is also the most important. If he still wants to be the most important, sooner or later he will become more aggressive.
All of the above is designed to show your dog that although he is an important member of the family, he is the least important member. As he grows up and accepts the household, it may be possible to adapt or relax some of the rules. Always bear in mind what he is learning and make sure that it is what you want.

It is a good idea to teach your dog not to push through doorways. You may choose to use a word such as "wait" for this.

quiz—analyzing
your dog's individual character

1. Does your dog learn:

a. quickly if it is to his advantage, slowly if you are trying to teach something?

b. very quickly?

c. quickly at home if there are no distractions, but becomes anxious if there is anything different around?

d. quickly if you are using rewards and fun, but moves away if you seem cross?

e. mostly quite quickly?

2. At home, is your dog:

a. very demanding of attention?

b. calm and settled?

c. quiet and introverted?

d. clingy and wanting to be in contact all the time?

e. affectionate, friendly, and settled most of the time?

We all have a different interpretation of a good relationship.

3. On walks, is your dog:

a. very active, ignoring you?

b. happy, responding perfectly to your wishes?

c. uncertain of anything new, tending to stay close to your side?

d. happy to be around but rushes back to you if something scares him?

e. happy and confident, responding well to your wishes, though not necessarily immediately?

4. How would you describe your dog?

a. A mind of his own, a great character?

b. The perfect dog?

c. Great if he is feeling confident, but upset in some situations?

d. Easily unsettled by raised voices, changes in routine or even your mood changes?

e. A great companion, but hard work sometimes?

Dogs vary in temperament as much as humans do. The important thing is to understand your own dog.

A dog may be lacking in confidence in certain situations but fully confident in others. For example, a dog may love people but be nervous around other dogs.

Mostly a's

You have a pushy dog. He is probably extremely clever, but maybe he is using his intelligence for his own gain. He needs to understand that you are both on the same side, a team, not in opposition. Try to work with him, rewarding good behavior so that he enjoys doing things for you.

Mostly b's

Either you have not been totally honest, in which case try again, or you are very lucky. You have the perfect dog. Well done. Some dogs are easier than others, some personalities get on better than others. Never take this for granted, it is a rare and wonderful thing.

Mostly c's

Your dog is lacking in confidence in some situations. Increase his socialization, but aim for gradual progress, do not overwhelm him. Make progress at his own pace.

Mostly d's

Your dog is sensitive. You probably have an extremely close relationship, but this type of dog can be easily upset by the ups and downs of family life. Make sure that you always reward good, confident behavior and resist the urge to cuddle him every time he looks anxious.

Mostly e's

Congratulations! You have achieved a good relationship with your dog. Dogs are rarely perfect all the time, especially when young. You understand this and expect good but not perfect behavior. Do not be tempted to sit back and assume all will be well. Keep working with your dog, having fun, and enjoying being with each other.

Mostly "I don't know"

It would seem that you do not know your dog very well at the moment. Spend more time with him, play with him, teach him things and let him teach you about him. Try the quiz again in another couple of weeks and compare the results.

Combinations of letters

Dogs rarely fit into distinct categories, so don't worry since this is not unusual. Read the relevant sections since your dog is showing a mixture of traits.

responsibilities
as a dog owner

Everybody wants a dog that can be enjoyed and causes no problems for anyone. As well as teaching our dogs the right behaviors, there are certain important responsibilities that come with dog ownership.

Poop scooping

Clearing up after your dog is one of the least pleasant aspects of dog ownership, but one that is essential. Whenever you are out with your dog, take a poop scoop or suitable plastic bag. If your dog makes a mess, clean it up! There are no exceptions.

Do not let your dog out on his own

Fortunately, it is now comparatively rare to see stray dogs as there are much tighter controls and legislation. It goes without saying that no dog should be out on his own, especially without a collar or leash.

Identification

Legally, your dog must wear a collar with an identification tag when he is out on the street. In addition, you could consider permanent identification systems such as tattooing and microchip implants. Speak to your own veterinarian for more details.

Neutering

Neutering is an issue that every dog owner should consider. *Spaying* a female means that she will no longer have seasons and cannot become pregnant. *Castrating* a male means the dog is no longer producing male hormones and cannot father unwanted puppies. Both these measures are helpful in preventing unwanted litters and therefore reducing the number of unwanted and badly treated dogs. Your dog may need slightly less food after the operation, but provided you balance food intake with exercise, there should be no problems with weight gain. Your dog will not lose his character. Spaying produces few behavioral

Poop scooping is an essential part of dog owning. If everyone cleaned up after their dogs, there would be a great deal less anti-dog feeling. Carry your bag with pride— your example may encourage others to be more responsible! Always carry a scoop or bag with you. Even if you don't need it someone else might!

Vacation Time

When you are going on vacation, plans must also be made for your dog. Is he coming with you? In which case, check for any restrictions and also that the place is suitable for your dog. Are you leaving him somewhere? Find out about reputable boarding kennels in plenty of time. Visit and ask questions before booking your dog in. Good kennels become busy and may not have a vacancy if you leave it too late. Perhaps a friend could look after your dog? You need to be sure that they will look after him properly.

changes, but it means that your bitch will not suffer mood swings associated with her season or false pregnancies, which can make her upset. Since castration takes away the male hormones, behaviors that are predominantly male, such as leg cocking, mounting, and tension towards other males, are usually reduced in most dogs. However, this reduction does depend on the age of the dog and how much of this behavior has already been learned by him.

There is evidence to suggest that neutered dogs actually live longer than dogs that have been left unneutered. Not only do these neutered dogs have much less desire to wander and go looking for females and males during their seasons, but they are less at risk from certain medical conditions such as pyometra and mammary tumours in the female, and prostate problems in the male.

Being left

Owning a dog is a huge responsibility, and you must think carefully about this before deciding to take that sweet puppy into your home. Once you become a dog owner, you have to consider your dog any time that you will be away from home for more than a short time. And this consideration should come before anything else. While most dogs learn to cope alone for up to a few hours, they cannot be left for extended periods. Apart from boredom and needing to empty themselves, they need company. Therefore, you must alter your routine to accommodate this. If you work full time, the neighbor who is pleased to look after your dog while you are on vacation may also be willing to come in during the day to keep your dog company and take him out for a walk.

excessive **barking**

Municipal authorities receive many complaints about barking, howling, and whining. Dogs make noises in order to communicate. You have to make sure that your dog does not inconvenience others with his vocalization. Make sure that your dog does not bark excessively when you are on walks or at home. Ask your neighbors to let you know if they hear your dog when you are out, or leave a tape recorder recording so that you can hear what happens. Your dog should not bark excessively in the yard or car. If there is a problem, read chapter 4.

Walks should be enjoyable for you and your dog whether on or off the leash. All dogs should accept walking on the leash and you should make sure that this forms part of your walks. If you know that your dog will not cause a problem for anyone, will remain under your control, and it is safe for him, off-leash exercise is wonderful for dogs.

If it is safe to let your dog off his leash, you must be certain that you have good control over your dog. If he is off his leash, he should not go out of your sight, since he then cannot be under your control.

Veterinary care

Owning a dog means regular veterinary visits. A healthy dog should not need too many visits, although he will need an annual checkup, and you should seek your vet's advice about booster vaccinations and routine worming. However,

Make sure that you can handle your dog all over and include this as part of a daily handling session.

Behavior toward others

Not all dogs have perfect manners at all times. If you feel that your dog could be a danger to anyone, it is your responsibility to prevent a situation from occurring. For more information on resolving problems, see chapter 4. In the short term, you must take steps to ensure your dog is safe. This may include shutting him away from workmen when they visit the house, keeping him on a leash on walks or explaining the situation to the veterinarian so that he knows to take extra care when handling your dog.

On walks

When walking your dog near traffic, he should be on a leash. Even if you feel certain your dog will not run into the road, he could be distracted.

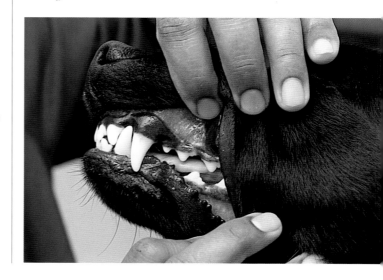

an accident, illness or approaching old age will mean more visits. This can be costly and time consuming. It may be a good idea to speak to your vet about veterinary insurance.

Your dog's general welfare

In addition to veterinary care, you are responsible for your dog's general welfare. This includes regular grooming. This varies with different dogs. Some longhaired breeds need daily grooming, whereas shorthaired dogs may simply need a daily check over and a thorough weekly grooming. Some breeds need specialist grooming treatment. Always check your dog's teeth and claws regularly, and make sure the area around his tail is clean.

Your dog and the law

Times are changing and there is more antidog feeling than there was 20 years ago. As a result, court cases are becoming increasingly common. If your dog misbehaves, you can be taken to court as a result. The Dangerous Dogs Act is one of the acts relating to dogs. *It applies to all dogs.* It is an offence for a dog to be dangerously out of control in a public place. The definition of all these terms can be quite loose. If found guilty, your dog can be destroyed and you can receive a criminal record as well as a large fine.

Advances in the veterinary world mean that many problems and diseases can be treated. Speak to your veterinarian if you have any concerns—do not wait until the problem is more established.

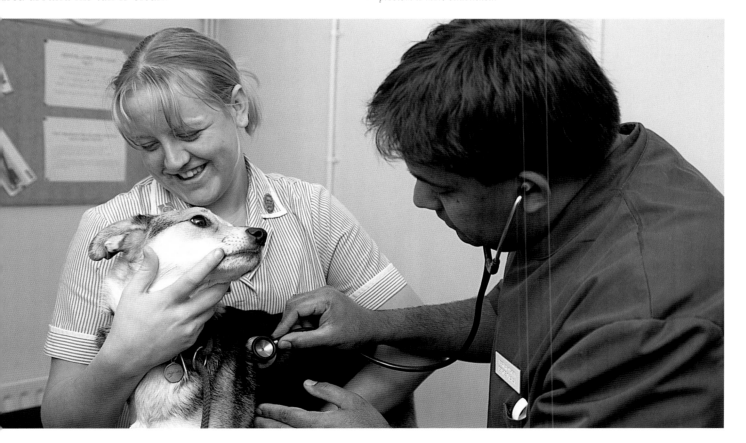

handling

Teaching your dog to accept being handled is essential.
• Each day you should check your dog over for lumps, bumps, cuts, thorns, etc.
• Your dog will need regular grooming.
• It is important that he accepts this from you, as part of his pack behavior.
• Not only will you need to handle your own dog, others will also have to handle him. This includes your veterinarian, kennel staff, show judges, friends, and so on. Start teaching him to accept this as soon as possible.

Begin with gentle stroking at a time when your dog is quiet and calm but not wanting to sleep. Make sure that you can stroke him all over, including his legs, tummy, mouth, and around his tail. This should not be a game or wrestling match. Reward with treats if this helps.

When you can stroke him all over, take a soft brush and stroke him with this. At first, stroke with the brush and give a treat. Then give two strokes with the brush for one treat, then three and so on. Keep sessions short and always end on a good note.

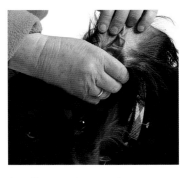 

As well as grooming your dog, you must pay particular attention to ears, eyes, claws, and teeth. You will then be able *to avoid many problems and if your dog does need treatment at any time, he will be used to being handled.*

Repeat using a towel. Do not wait until your dog is wet or muddy, practice when he is dry. Stroke one paw with the towel and stop and reward him for good behavior. This way he learns to be more tolerant. Progress to being able to brush your dog all over, pick up his feet, open his mouth, dry him with a towel, adjust his collar and anything else. Ideally, other members in the family should also repeat this process. It may help to have a certain area for brushing, but your dog should learn to tolerate handling everywhere.

If possible, it is a good idea to teach your dog to accept being lifted up. Practice in the house and also when you are out, since it may be necessary to do this sometime. Make sure that your dog does not find this frightening or threatening and that he is not in danger of being dropped.

Life Skills

Handling Correctly

Handling is not a game. Play with your dog frequently but not during handling sessions. If your dog learns that mouthing and wriggling mean that he gets his own way and the session finishes, he will use this in other situations. You will have to handle him every day throughout his life. Isn't it easier to invest the time now to teach him how to behave properly? It is not a good idea to give your dog an old towel or brush to play with or chew on. How will he know the difference between grooming and playtime?

If you have a dog whose coat needs a great deal of care, speak to others with the same breed, and a grooming parlor for advice. Make sure that your dog is happy to be picked up if appropriate for his size, or legs lifted if not. Being able to brush your dog's teeth is also a good idea. Dog toothbrushes and toothpaste are available from many pet stores and vets.

Practice handling your dog outside—this is extremely useful if he cuts himself or becomes tangled in undergrowth. Ask friends to handle your dog sometimes, so that he is not surprised when others need to touch him.

If you only dry your dog when he is wet, it is difficult to teach him how to behave. Practice drying one foot at a time when he is not wet or muddy. Reward good behavior.

Left: Some dogs need special attention to some parts of their body, so ensure that they are happy for you to handle these areas frequently.

Left: Once your dog is happy for you to handle him, gradually introduce gentle brushing.

having fun
with your dog

Games

Games are one of the most important ways we have of communicating with our dogs. Dogs learn through games and so although they enjoy them, games are not "just for fun." You have control over what games your dog plays and it is up to you whether your dog learns the right or wrong things. Remember, games are also a great way for a dog to find out who is controlling whom, so make sure that you are the one in control. There are many different varieties of games that dogs and their owners can play. Here are some types of games that you can play with your dog.

Dog chasing a toy

This game has been played by dogs and their owners for as long as dogs have been pets. The owner throws the toy, the dog runs after the toy. The dog may pick up the toy, bring it back to the owner, and give it to him. A simple game of fetch is great, it provides good exercise, and many dogs love it. You can teach him to bring the toy to you, to put it in your hand, and so on. However, the dog may begin to play a game of possession.

Chasing is a natural instinct and some dogs show this more than others. Here, a dog needs to chase and in the absence of more natural prey, chases the wheelbarrow. If he hasn't been taught the rules, this can be difficult to stop.

Be careful, some dogs can begin to learn the wrong things. If this game is played too much without control, a dog can learn to run after anything that moves, including other dogs, children, joggers and bikes or cars. Therefore it is a good idea to play the game, but to teach control, so that you can call your dog back when you choose (see chapter 3).

Herding dogs, such as Border Collies and sheepdogs, usually excel at this type of game.

Possession

Dogs develop two versions of this game.

Game One involves the owner holding the toy. This then becomes a "tug-of-war" with dog and owner tugging furiously. Quite often, one or both will begin to growl. This type of game is highly motivating for the dog.

But, take great care. If your dog is controlling these games, he could be learning to growl at you and to pit his strength against yours. Make sure that you can stop the game and take the toy away from him at any time. If you

cannot do this, it is best to avoid playing this game until you have developed greater control.

Game Two involves the dog holding the toy and preventing the owner from getting it. The dog usually "teases" the owner into playing and the owner accommodates by then chasing the dog.

Again, if this game is not under your control, your dog will be learning the wrong thing. Make sure that you can get him to come to you when you ask. Play in an enclosed space, maybe even with a leash or long line on your dog. When he comes to you, reward him for coming first, before trying to take the toy. Teach him to give up the toy for a reward. Again, if there are difficulties or if your dog won't give up objects, avoid this game until you have more control.

Many people think that exercising two dogs together will be half the work for the owner. This is seldom the case, since games between dogs can get out of hand. Play with both dogs separately rather than simply letting them play together all the time.

rough games
with a person

Rough and tumble can be fun, increase confidence, and help a dog to become accustomed to being handled. But it is a game that can lead to problems. It often teaches a dog the wrong habits, such as mouthing and jumping up. It can teach him that he is more powerful and agile than you. The game can easily get out of hand and can teach a dog to be aggressive. Generally, the type of dog who wants to play these games is the type who should not. It is a game best avoided with many dogs

Activity toys mean that dogs can occupy themselves for short periods of time without you. They are especially beneficial for young dogs, energetic dogs, and dogs learning to be left alone.

except in a very calm, gentle way. Even then, it must be on the owner's terms with strict rules. Confident, pushy dogs often like these games. For some reason, so do many male members of the family!

Games on his own

Very few dogs play on their own. They may play for an audience because they enjoy the reaction, but many dogs are not interested unless someone is there to play with.

There is a range of toys available that comes under the heading of "activity toys." These are usually quite sturdy and are designed to have food inserted. Your dog then manouvers the toy with his paws, nose and mouth to obtain the food. They are a great way to give your dog extra stimulation. These toys include hard plastic balls and cubes to put dried food in, and softer rubber toys to stuff with wet food, or to insert biscuits into other specially shaped holes.

However, these toys should not be your dog's only source of fun. They should be in addition to games with you, not instead of. Do not leave a toy with your dog if he could destroy it and maybe swallow parts of it. Do not give it to him if it makes him frustrated and annoyed. These toys are best avoided with dogs who are possessive over food. If you have more than one dog, take extra care since some dogs will guard food from others.

Clever dogs often benefit from extra stimulation, along with dogs who have to be left and those with busy owners. This section is not designed to put you off playing games with your dog. In fact, the opposite should be the case, since games are so important. However, do be aware of what your dog is learning and which games are most appropriate for him, at his stage of learning.

Games with Another Dog

Watching two dogs play nicely together is wonderful. It gives lots of exercise and can enhance social skills.

But be careful. Games can get out of hand and dogs can learn to fight this way. It is possible that you will experience difficulty in controlling your dog. Different dogs have different ideas about games—your dog's games may be too rough for another dog, or he may meet someone who plays much more roughly than he does. You must be the most important thing in your dog's life and his optimum game partner.

rules of the
game

Whatever games are played, you should enforce a set of simple rules.

No mouthing

Mouthing people or clothing is not allowed. Encourage your dog to hold a toy to make him less likely to do this, and play calmer games.

No jumping up

Whatever he learns in a game, he will exhibit at other times. Therefore, if he jumps at you and you throw the toy, he will jump up at other times too. Teach him that having four feet on the ground is what brings the reward of the game continuing. If he is likely to jump, teach him to sit down and keep still instead.

No snatching the toy

Basic manners mean that he should not try to grab the toy.

Have different toys for different games. Some toys may be left with your dog, while you keep others for games which you initiate.

Teach to give up the toy when asked

In order to teach your dog to give things to you, you must give him a good reason to do so. Do not try to grab the toy, as this will make him hold on harder. Instead, reward him for coming to you, then produce something interesting, such as a treat or another toy. Make this really interesting by giving it lots of attention. When your dog drops his toy, tell him he is wonderful, pick it up and reward him with the treat or a game with the second toy. The word "give" should begin to mean "spit that out quickly, as I have something much more interesting."

No teasing

You are asking your dog to abide by your rules, but you must also consider him. Therefore, teasing him is not allowed, neither is anything he finds unpleasant.

If the dog breaks the rules, it is the end of the game

If at any time, the dog breaks any of your rules, simply stop the game, having removed the toy first if possible. Walk away and ignore your dog. He will soon learn that all fun stops if he breaks the rules. Next time, play calmer, more gentle games to help your dog understand what you want.

Any other rules

Certain circumstances will need extra thought. If you have young children or elderly people in the household, or if your dog is especially large or powerful, you may need to impose extra precautions. No barking is a particularly good rule for noisy dogs.

Toys

There are lots of different types of toys around. Do not feel that you have to spend a fortune on the latest toy. Look around and use toys that appeal to you and your dog. Try to have a variety so that you and your dog can play different games. There are tough toys that are suitable for many dogs. There are toys sold as indestructible, which are great for boisterous and energetic dogs.

Games involving strength and possession are not the best ones to play unless you know that the dog will drop the toy when you ask.

Toys must always be safe for your dog. If you are in any doubt, either remove the toy or only let him have it under supervision.

Safety

Safety is essential. Depending on your dog, his age, size, personality, and the game being played, different toys will be suitable. Check toys regularly for wear and tear and replace when necessary.

Other games

See pp. 72–75 for games to channel your dog's mental and physical energies.

things to do
with your dog

In addition to playing games, there are lots of ways of enjoying your dog.

The following are some suggestions. Not all will be suitable for all dogs, so do not try something that would not be in the best interests of you or your dog.

In general, a friendly, well-adjusted, well-behaved dog with an enthusiastic, sensible owner will be able to enjoy more situations than a dog who is antisocial or badly behaved. You know your own dog. What would he enjoy?

1. Walks

Walking your dog should form part of your daily life together. Walks should fulfill at least two functions.

a. Education and socialization. This includes road walking, meeting other dogs, going out and about, and generally learning about how to behave in different social situations.

b. Releasing energy. This is when your dog is able to move more quickly, run, play, and sniff. This is his time to be a dog and to use up some of his energy. If it is not appropriate for him to be off his leash, you must be more inventive in finding outlets for his energy.

2. Sponsored walks

You may find details of a local sponsored dog walk. For sociable people and dogs, this can be a great day. If there are none locally, perhaps you could think about organizing one of your own.

3. Dog shows

Many people enjoy attending dog shows. However, you do not need to own a champion to compete. Exemption and Fun dog shows have classes for all dogs, not just pedigrees. There will be novelty classes such as "the dog with the waggiest tail" and "dog in best condition."

Left: During each walk, have some time for teaching your dog and some time when he can use up his energies, play, sniff, etc.

Below: Dog shows are something which many people and dogs enjoy. There are events for all levels, from the interested pet owner to the dedicated show enthusiast.

Agility is important for energetic dogs and owners. Look around for classes which teach this.

The Danger of Hot Cars

TAKE CARE. Dogs should never be left in hot cars, as they can easily overheat. Even when you are traveling, a car can become too hot for your dog, especially if he is surrounded by glass, such as in a hatchback. If in doubt, leave your dog at home.

---

3. Car travel

Lots of dogs like accompanying their owners on car trips. Provided that the weather is not too hot or too cold, this should be no problem. Make sure that your dog travels safely and does not jump around or bark since this can be dangerous for both dog and driver.

4. Visiting friends

If you have a sociable, well-behaved dog, it is likely that you will have friends who would be happy for him to visit with you. If you have started the habit when he was a puppy, he should have no problems learning the rules of friends' houses.

5. Training classes

A good training class should be interesting and fun for you and your dog. Find out about classes in your area. In addition to general pet dog training, you may be interested in one of the competitive sports associated with dogs, such as agility, flyball, working trials or obedience.

6. Weekend courses

Read the dog magazines for details of weekend courses that you can attend with your dog. Several places offer these throughout the summer, and sometimes individual courses are arranged. These can be a great way of learning new skills with your dog, enjoying each other's company, and meeting new friends.

Training classes specialize in teaching different things. There are classes for pet dogs, obedience, ringcraft, and others.

7. Activity vacations

If you enjoy this sort of thing, look in the dog press for details of organized vacations that you could possibly attend with your dog.

8. Vacations

If you fancy something less structured, how about taking your dog on vacation with you? Many hotels, self-catering accommodations, caravans, and campsites allow well-behaved dogs. Make inquiries first to insure that your dog is allowed and that the place will be suitable for him.

9. Friends' dogs visiting

If your dog is sociable, try having a friend's dog over for a few hours. Make sure that the dogs are good friends away from the home first. Then take care. Some dogs are territorial around their own home. If there are problems, abandon the idea. However, if it works, it can be great fun for the dogs and a useful idea if you are out for the day and would like someone to look after your dog.

10. Swimming

Many dogs love swimming. If the idea of a cold river does not appeal, make investigations to find out if there is a "dog swimming pool" within traveling distance. These specially heated pools offer a safe place for water fun and are extremely good for some dogs who have to be careful about exercise. Speak to your vet if you are unsure about whether this is suitable for your dog.

Some dogs, such as this Newfoundland, love to swim. However, don't be put off, you do not have to go in the water with them unless you want to.

An organization such as PAT Dogs means that other people can get to know and love your dog too.

11. PAT dogs

There is a UK charity called Pro-Dogs which has developed an idea known as Pets As Therapy, or PAT Dogs. These are pet dogs who have been specially assessed. They then visit nursing homes, residential homes, hospitals, and similar places with their owners for the residents to meet and stroke the dogs. Owners find this highly rewarding, the residents have the opportunity to spend time with a friendly dog, and the dogs are made to feel wonderful.

12. Racing

These events are held at some greyhound racing stadiums and are open to all dogs. They are purely for fun and are entirely separate from the serious greyhound races.

13. Visiting the pub

Check in advance that dogs are welcome. What a great way to help socialize your dog!

14. Country fairs and shows

If dogs are allowed, these are a good way of socializing your dog and there are often fun events such as a fun race, scurry, or obstacle course which you could enter.

15. Stay at home and enjoy comfort and warmth with a sleepy dog to keep you company

Dogs are great fun. You do not need to rush around all the time, simply enjoy being with your dog!

Things for your dog to do without you

Although quality time with your dog is important, you cannot spend all your time with him. Therefore, giving him things that he can enjoy without us is important. Read the section on activity toys. There are many toys or safe bones that can be stuffed with food which your dog can enjoy licking out. Try rubbing the toys first with something sticky and tasty, such as cream cheese or peanut butter.

training for life

3

Training your dog—for many people, the very phrase conjures up images of military types bellowing commands to a group of confused dogs and owners on a cold, wet field! However, this is not what we are talking about.

Training with your dog should be a two-way process, with communication between you both. Training will enable you to enjoy your dog more fully. We do not want a dog who, robotlike, obeys every command, we want a dog we can enjoy taking places with us. A dog who comes when he is called can be let off his leash in safe places to run. A dog who walks nicely on a leash can enjoy day trips with the family. A dog who settles down in the house can meet visitors and enjoy their company. A well-trained dog can enjoy sharing life with the family, without needing to be excluded.

how dogs **learn**

Dogs learn very quickly. There is one rule:

If a dog finds an action rewarding, he is much more likely to repeat it and keep repeating it.

Almost everything your dog does will be based on this.

What is rewarding?

Anything he enjoys. This could include gaining attention, getting a treat, playing a game, running around, meeting other people and dogs, going to sleep; it all depends on what he wants at the time.

Therefore, as long as we remember the rule, training becomes much easier.

When teaching, we could try to *make* our dogs do something. The old type of training involved pulling and pushing our dogs.

The new methods of motivational training are based on making our dogs *want* to do it. There are many advantages.

- It is much more fun for dogs and owners.
- Since it does not rely on strength or brute force, everyone, even the very young, can get results this way.
- It uses the dog's natural instincts.
- It is usually quicker, since the dog understands the owner and wants to learn.

In order to reward our dog, we need to know what it is that he finds rewarding, and will therefore be more likely to repeat.
What it is that your dog likes best? Most rewards that we can give our dogs fall into one of four basic categories.

Once we understand how dogs learn, everyone can be involved in teaching the dog. These methods involve working with the dog's mind, not forcing the body.

Find out what treats your dog likes best, and what works most effectively in different situations. Use lots of treats when training, but make sure that he still has a well-balanced diet.

1. Food

This is probably the most useful group. It does help if you have a greedy dog, but it is not essential. Find your dog's favorite food and divide it into tiny sections. If you are using meat or cheese, cut it into pieces roughly the size of your little finger nail. Each of these is one reward.

Ensure that whatever you give to your dog is safe for him in small quantities. Human chocolate is not a good idea since it can be toxic for dogs. Meat, cheese, bread, and cat treats are all possibilities. Many commercial dog treats are far too large to be used in training.

Think of other food your dog enjoys that can be used as a lesser reward. For example, he may enjoy pieces of one of the dried foods or dog biscuits. These can usually be used in larger quantities, thus saving the best treats for teaching new or difficult exercises.

Adjust your dog's food accordingly. We do not want him to become overweight or receive an unbalanced diet. Therefore, set aside a handful of his dried food for use as treats during the day.

At first, you will use lots of rewards, but as time goes on, these should be reduced, since your dog will begin to understand what it is you want him to do.

2. Games

Games are a good way of increasing motivation. They are a good way of developing the bond that will help training, for example encouraging your dog to come when you call him. However, they are not so good for teaching the exercises where your dog does not move, like sitting and staying. Your dog is then more likely to move in anticipation of his game. Therefore, use games for training only when appropriate.

Many dogs love to play, but most need encouraging to play the games you choose and they need to learn the rules.

3. Attention

Your attention is a big reward for your dog, but often it is not as powerful as the motivation to do something else, like going to play with another dog. Because we love our dogs and enjoy their company, we tend to give them lots of free attention. We talk to them and fuss them just for being there. There is nothing wrong with this, but do not expect your dog to work for the reward that he knows he can get for free later. Therefore, use verbal and physical praise, but in conjunction with other rewards, such as food, especially when teaching your dog something new or difficult.

Life Skills

Timing

Rewards are essential, but so is timing. A dog views the consequences of his action as the time during or immediately after the action.

Imagine: you ask your dog to sit, he sits and you rummage in your pocket for a treat. However, by the time you give the treat to your dog, he is already standing again. What has your dog learned? To sit? Or to stand? He will associate the reward with the last thing he did. If instead of standing, he jumped up at you, you are now teaching him to jump up.

Therefore, the reward must be during or immediately after the action. With a young or untrained dog, this timing is vitally important, since a delay of more than half a second can mean that he is learning something else.

Most dogs love attention from their owner and so you can use this to your advantage.

Food is often useful to lure your dog into positions when training, but remember to use other rewards, especially as he progresses.

4. Access to something he wants

Imagine your dog wants to go out into the yard. He scratches at the door, you get up, and open it. Your dog has learned that scratching at the door means you are more likely to open it and he will repeat this action. Is that what you want? You can use these situations to help teach him to respond to you. Before opening the door, ask him to sit if you have taught him the word. When he does, praise him and open the door. This way, your dog learns that he can earn the things he wants through good behavior.

5. Punishment

As human beings, we are sometimes extremely quick to resort to punishment, despite the overwhelming evidence that it can actually slow down learning. It can also damage the relationship between dog and owner which in turn inhibits further learning.

A dog will do what is most rewarding; therefore, how can punishment teach a dog to do things for us? Even if punishment can stop one behavior (and there is evidence to show that this is not necessarily the case), how does that tell the dog what we are wanting?

If he gets something wrong, maybe this is because he is confused or doesn't understand, rather than that he is just "being naughty." If this is the case, how will punishment help?

Rewards will teach our dog almost all that he needs to know. If he is making a mistake, we need to look at other ways of explaining what we want, rather than becoming angry.

the principles of **reward based training**

Golden rules for teaching a dog

1. Start now
The best age to start training is now. However young your puppy is, however old your dog is, it is never too early or too late.

2. Learn from your dog
As we stated at the beginning, training should be a two-way communication. You must be willing to learn from your dog. The more you learn about him, the easier training will become.

The aim of training is to have a well-behaved dog that you can take with you to different places, enjoy his company, and be sure that he causes no problems for anyone else. It means that you and your dog can enjoy more things together.

3. Have short sessions
Do not expect your dog to concentrate for long. Like us, the more difficult something is, the shorter the time he can concentrate. At first, aim for sessions of between half a minute and two minutes. As you and your dog begin to understand each other better, the time can be extended so long as you are both enjoying it. Lots of short sessions throughout each day will help your dog learn much more quickly than one long session where you both become tired, confused and bored.

4. Have fun
Dogs are like us in that they learn best when something is enjoyable. Make sessions fun and rewarding, and you and your dog will want to learn together. If you start, then realize that you or your dog is simply not in "the mood," expect less and end the session early.

5. A stressed dog will not learn
If your dog is feeling anxious, he will not be able to learn, especially if you are expecting too much of him. If he is in an environment that worries him, such as close to a bouncy dog, heavy traffic, or too many people, he may find it difficult to cope with.

6. Begin and end on a good note
As your training sessions become a little longer, always start with something familiar to your dog, to help him settle. Similarly, do something easy or enjoyable before finishing a session.

7. All the family should be involved
In the days of old, only one person was advised to train a dog to avoid confusion. However, we need a pet dog to

When using reward based training, the whole family can be involved since the methods are fun and easy.

respond to all members of the family. Therefore, everyone should be involved to whatever extent is appropriate, under close supervision when necessary. If someone in the family is not involved with training the dog, do not be surprised if the dog does not respond to them.

8. Be consistent

Dogs cannot learn what we want if we do not teach them. If we vary the words we use, and different people have different expectations, our dog will simply become confused and disinclined to play this training game with us. He will begin to make his own decisions or try to guess what we want. We owe it to him to make it as easy as possible for him to understand.

9. Teach—do not expect him to know

Dogs do not understand English, therefore they cannot know what we mean unless we have taught them. If you feel that you have taught something, and your dog is still not responding as he should, instead of blaming him for being naughty, ask yourself how you can teach him more effectively. He obviously has not learned what you wanted, so start again to help him.

Watch how dogs and puppies communicate with each other and use this to help you understand your own dog better and therefore to make training easier.

Begin training where there are few distractions and progress to teaching in all different circumstances. Use better rewards when an exercise is more difficult for him.

10. Train in different places and times

If you only train your dog in your front room, standing at his side, just before dinner, it is likely that this will be the only time your dog responds to you. Instead, teach throughout the day, at all different times, places, and situations.

Teaching in the house will be easier, so do this first, then progress to teaching the same things outside.

11. Success brings success

If we are successful at something we do, we are more likely to enjoy doing it and will make the decision to repeat it. A dog is just like us—if he achieves success, he will try again. A dog who is not successful is not rewarded. Therefore he becomes confused and uncertain and less likely to enjoy being with you.

12. Gradually increase distractions

When teaching something new, have as few distractions around as possible. Gradually increase the distractions so that your dog still wants to do things for you, no matter who else is around. For example, when first teaching your dog to sit, do this in a quiet part of the house, when no one else is around. Once he understands this, begin to do it in different places and when others are moving around. Then try outside, when there are no distractions. Progress to being able to ask your dog to sit during a walk when there are other dogs and people around.

13. Use rewards effectively

We need to build our dog's motivation. Whenever anything is difficult or new, use especially important rewards. As your dog progresses and begins to understand what you want, and wants to do it for you, vary the rewards to include less exciting ones, decrease them, and give them on a random basis.

14. Tone of voice

Old-type training involved bellowing and yelling in order to show authority. As we know from the previous chapter, this is not necessary and can teach a dog not to listen. When

A great deal of training can be practised from a comfy chair!

Always try to see the situation from your dog's point of view. What is he learning?

Are you giving cues which he has noticed and you have failed to?

Does he understand what you want him to do?

You ask your dog to do something, you must mean it. There is no point asking him to sit if you do not care whether he does or not. If this is the case, don't say anything. Talk in your normal tone of voice, clearly and in such a way that you feel he will respond.

15. Do not repeat words

If your dog is listening and wants to respond, you only have to use the word he knows once. If you are repeating yourself, it means your dog is not listening, does not want to do it, or does not understand. Find out why he is not responding and work on this, rather than saying the same thing over and over again.

16. What is he learning?

At all times, be aware of what your dog is learning. You should know what you are trying to teach, but is this what your dog is learning? If so, continue, but keep checking. If your dog is not learning what you want, you need to alter your approach in order to be successful.

clicker *training*

A clicker is a training tool, which is rapidly gaining popularity. It establishes a system of communication between you and your dog that cuts through the language barrier and can make training easier.

What is it?

A clicker is a small plastic item, shaped like a box, with a piece of metal inside. When the metal is pressed, it makes a "click-click" sound.

How do I use it?

The clicker is a signal that your dog has just done the right thing and a reward is coming.

How does my dog know this?

To begin with, take a handful of tasty treats, click, and then immediately give your dog a treat. You are not asking him to do anything at this stage, just teaching him that the sound of the click means a reward is about to follow. Once your dog has made this association, you can then begin to use it in your training. As soon as your dog has done the right thing, click. You then have an extra few seconds to give him the reward.

What are the benefits?

There are several:

- The sound is clear to your dog and therefore it helps him to avoid confusion and to learn.
- All members of the family can use it, so training is consistent.
- Once the timing of the click is accurate, you have a little extra time to produce the reward.

Advanced training can be made easier by using a clicker.

How do we progress?

As with any other type of training, you gradually ask your dog to work harder for each reward, or, in this case, each click and reward.

What if my dog ignores the click?

This just means that he has not made the association that a click predicts something good. Click and treat him several more times, making sure that the treats are something he really enjoys.

What if my dog is afraid of the click?

This sometimes happens. You could try muffling the click by holding it in your hand and wearing a glove. Otherwise, it may be best to avoid the clicker, and look for another noise to use instead.

Do I need a clicker?

No, not necessarily. Many people, and dogs, find that it helps, but some people find that it is simply something

extra to think about. Use whatever suits you and your dog.

Where can I get a clicker from?

Some pet stores sell them. Many dog trainers, behavior counselors and training clubs will also have them. They will also be able to give you individual guidance on using it with your dog.

Use of a clicker can simplify training for you and your dog.

Final Point

Use the Clicker Carefully

Before using a clicker, put it close to your ear and click. It is not pleasant, is it? Remember this and never use one right beside your dog's ear.

The exercises in this book talk about rewarding the dog. The type of reward will depend on what you and your dog find most effective. If you are using clicker training, the reward is "click," followed by an appropriate reward. If not using a clicker, use a reward appropriate to the exercise.

step-by-step exercises
teaching your dog

This sequence should be followed for each of the exercises detailed in this section.

1. Be certain of what it is that you want to teach.

2. Begin in a relatively quiet environment, free from distractions.

3. Show your dog a piece of really interesting food.

4. Use this as a lure to show your dog what you want. Be patient and avoid pulling or pushing him around. Instead, find ways to encourage him to do it himself.

5. As soon as your dog does as you want, reward him with the food and a fuss.

6. At this stage, do not give your dog any words of command.

7. Repeat several times, until your dog is performing the action reliably, then begin to say your word as the dog is doing the action.

8. Show the dog the treat and say your word. Lure him if necessary. Reward him.

9. Progress so that you can say the word and the dog will repeat the action without needing to follow your hand.

10. Start varying the rewards. Use a different or less interesting reward sometimes, or have the treat in your hand but only give him a fuss and praise as reward. At other times, do not have the treat in your hand, but suddenly produce one from the other hand as soon as he does what you ask.

11. Rewards should now come on a random basis. Gradually vary and decrease the rewards given. This means that your dog does not know when he will be rewarded, or with what type of reward—he needs to do as you ask to find out what he will get.

12. Repeat this sequence in different places, with an increasing number of distractions, for example in different rooms in the house, in the yard, on a leash on the sidewalk, in a field with no one around. Progress to a field with other dogs and people around, and your house when visitors are there.

Using words

Dogs do not understand English and will only understand what we teach them. Therefore, the accuracy of your dog's response will depend on how effectively you teach him. We need to make life as easy as possible for him. He is now learning our language.

One word must equal one action. We know that one word can have a variety of meanings, but how can our dog

Once your dog understands what you want, train in different places and gradually increase the distractions.

"What do you mean 'down,' I am lying down!"

understand this? What does "down" mean? Lie down, get down, come down, sit down? You decide for your dog. Everyone in the family must be consistent and use the same words. It is no good if one person says "down" to mean lie down and someone else says "down" to mean don't jump up.

Take a blank piece of paper—this will be your dog's dictionary. Write down each word you teach your dog, along with the meaning, and pin it somewhere obvious, where everyone will be reminded by it. Add to the list as you progress and teach more words.

1. getting your dog's attention

The first thing is to get your dog's attention. It may sound obvious, but so many people miss this step. It is the most important thing you can teach your dog, since you need him to *want* to listen to you. If his mind is elsewhere, he will not learn. Throughout his entire life, if you are ever having difficulties, come back to this basic principle. Can you get your dog's attention? If not, you are likely to experience some difficulties in that situation.

If your dog does not want to listen to you, training becomes extremely difficult.

Therefore, we will work through the sequence on the previous page.

1. What are you teaching? You want to teach your dog that when you say his name, it means "look at me, something interesting is going to happen."

2. Begin in a relatively quiet environment, free from distractions. Find a quiet place.

3. Show your dog a piece of really interesting food. Have some treats in a small pot or in a pocket, out of your dog's reach, holding only one piece in your hand at any time.

4. Use this as a lure to show your dog what you want. Find ways to encourage him to do it himself. Your dog should now be looking at you. Well done, he has already been successful.

5. As soon as your dog does as you want, reward him with the food and a fuss. Reward him.

6. At this stage, do not give your dog any words of command.

7. Repeat several times until your dog is performing the action reliably. Then begin to say your word as the dog is doing the action. Begin to say his name before rewarding him.

8. Show your dog the treat and say your word. Reward him. No lures are necessary, just repeat several times.

9. Progress until you can say the word and your dog will repeat the action without following your hand. This should be easy to achieve.

10. Start varying the rewards. Use a different or less interesting reward sometimes; at other times, have the treat in your hand but give him only a fuss and praise as reward, as soon as he does what you ask. Continue to practice.

11. Gradually and randomly vary and decrease the rewards given. **This means that your dog does not know when or with what he will be rewarded. He needs to respond to find out.** Your dog should be confident that his name means "look at me to find out what nice things we are going to do together."

12. Progress to repeating this sequence in different places with an increasing number of distractions:

- In the house:
• with no distractions
• when a visitor has been here for a little while
• when a visitor first arrives
• when the doorbell rings

- On a walk:
• with no distractions
• with a person or dog in the distance
• with a person or dog nearby
• when greeting a person or dog

- In the car and in the yard

Practicing in different situations is so important. If you find that your dog cannot look at you when you ask, it is unlikely he will be able to do anything else for you. Always go back to this simple premise, which you taught your puppy right from the start.

Being able to get your dog's attention is a little like finding his "on" switch. Without it, you can do very little.

2. coming when called

Being able to experience freedom, run around, and explore is all part of being a dog. However, this can only be provided if it is safe. Safety means not only a suitable environment, but also a dog who will respond to you. If your dog does not want to be with you, how do you expect him to learn from you?

• In the house, get someone to hold your dog. Show him a treat or toy and rush away, calling him to you. The other person should let go. Make a huge fuss of your dog and give him the treat or have a game when he reaches you.

• Outside, with your dog on a leash, repeat as above. The other person should hold the leash, as you rush away. When you call the dog, they must keep hold of the leash and run with the dog until he gets to you. Reward him.

• Say your dog's name and show him a treat. Run backwards, still holding the leash, but not so tightly that it is pulling him, and encourage your dog to follow. He must

Teach in the house at first. It should be a fun exercise which your dog enjoys.

Other Points

• Never chase your dog. This will make him run away from you. Instead, run away from him. This will make you even more interesting to him.

• Never call your dog to you for anything unpleasant, either in or out of the house. This could include when you give him a bath, or take something out of his mouth.

• Never be angry with your dog when he does return to you. He will associate this with the last thing he did which was coming to you. Anything unpleasant will simply make him stay away for longer next time. However you are feeling, you must be nice to your dog when he comes to you.

• You must be the most interesting thing to your dog, even on walks. Play games, be fun!

• Never take it for granted that your dog will always come when you call him. It is very hard for a dog to choose returning to you above sniffing, playing or running. Always reward him.

The end result of this training should be a dog who will reliably, and happily, come back when you call him.

come of his own accord. After a few steps, stop and reward him for stopping with you.

• Repeat in different places, with increasing distractions.

• As you become more confident in a safe area, you can drop the leash as your dog begins to run towards you.

• As he progresses, you can allow him increased freedom in safe places. Call him several times during the walk, reward him, and let him go again. This applies whether he is on or off the leash. If he is off the leash, call him to you, put the leash on, reward him, and let him free again. This way he knows that coming to you means more fun, not the end of it. At the end of the walk, call your dog, put the leash on, have a great game, then go home.

Even if you do not let your dog off his leash for whatever reason, it is important to teach this exercise. If he did ever get out on his own, or if the leash broke, you need to know that he will return to you.

A long line or extending leash means that you can allow your dog more freedom while you teach him in open places.

3. walking on a loose leash

Walks will be more pleasant for both of you if your dog walks nicely on a leash. In this instance, although treats may help, the reward your dog wants is that you continue with your progress. Remember, your dog wants to get there and humans move more slowly than dogs.

The walk starts as soon as the leash is picked up. Only reward the behavior that you wish your dog to repeat. Therefore, if your dog is leaping around, do not progress until he is calmer. Then try again. As soon as the leash is attached to your dog, stand still. If your dog pulls forward, gently bring him back to your side and loosen the leash. If he pulls again, repeat. When he is standing at your side, on a loose leash, reward him by taking a

step forward. Then stand still. If he is pulling, repeat the above. Only take a step forward when he is standing calmly at your side, on a loose leash.

This is time-consuming. Be patient and consistent. Remember to practice. For some reason, although we practice teaching our dog to sit and lie down, we think that our dog should learn to walk on a leash during his walks. This makes life harder for everyone. Spend a few minutes teaching your dog how to walk nicely on a leash. Practice around the house, in the driveway, on the street, and when you go out for a walk. There is a great deal of learning that can take place before you and your dog even get out of your front door.

If your dog is pulling before you open the door, do not be surprised if he

If you find it difficult to put the leash on your dog because he is excited, do not be surprised if you cannot control him when he is on the leash. Take the time to teach the right behavior from the very beginning of a walk.

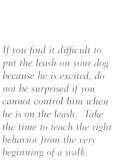

As well as being uncomfortable for you, pulling can cause pain and even permanent damage to your dog.

continues to pull during the rest of the walk. If you are having difficulties, stop when your dog pulls, bring him back to your side, and try one of the following:

• Stand still and wait.

• Loosen the leash, and repeat until he will wait with you.

• Ask your dog to look at you and reward this.

• Ask your dog to sit, and reward him.

• Walk backwards.

• Turn around and walk in the opposite direction.

• Walk in a small circle.

• Do not allow your dog to dictate where you are going.

The aim of all this is to teach your dog that progress will only be made when he is at your side on a loose leash. If he pulls, progress slows down. Therefore, it is in his best interest to stay at your side.

The equipment you use on your dog can make a difference. Harnesses and headcollars can be a great help. They will not teach your dog, but they can be helpful for him while you teach.

Do not be unpleasant to your dog. The aim is to teach him that the best place is to be by your side. This cannot be achieved by threatening, pulling, jerking, or shouting.

Old-style training relied on the use of jerking the dog around on a choke chain. Fortunately, enlightened thinking has meant that this is now an outdated method. Not only was it generally ineffective and unpleasant, it caused physical problems with dogs.

Train your dog in all situations. Road safety is always important.

He should only move to cross a road when you tell him to.

Make sure that he's doing what you want, not what he wants.

Walks become easier, more enjoyable and safer when your dog is under your control.

4. sit

Teaching a dog to sit when you ask should be one of the simplest training exercises.

We will work through the procedure that was outlined previously.

1. What are you teaching? The aim is to teach your dog to sit when you ask him. 'Sit' means *"put your back end on the floor and something really good may happen."*
Watch your dog when he sits of his own accord. As well as his back end touching the floor, his head moves upwards and backwards.

2. Begin in a relatively quiet environment, free of distractions. Have a jar of tasty treats out of your dog's reach. Make sure you have one in your hand.

3. Show your dog a piece of really interesting food. Make sure that you have his attention.

4. Use this as a lure to show your dog what you want.
Put the treat close to your dog's nose. Move it just above. Slowly, move the treat backwards, toward the top of your dog's head.
If you move the treat too high, your dog will jump up.

Lure your dog with food at the beginning, but reduce your hand signals as you progress, and then begin using different rewards. This way, you have a dog who wants to respond to you, rather than only responding when you are holding food.

If you move it too low he cannot move.
If you move it too fast he will walk backwards.
Be patient. If he does the wrong thing, just try again.
Keep his interest but do not give him the treat until he does the right thing.

Do not push his back end down. Not only does this cause discomfort for some dogs, he will at best simply learn to let you do this, which teaches him nothing, and at worst, he will learn to resist you and push upwards.

8. Show the dog the treat and say your word. Lure him if necessary. Reward him. At the moment, your dog is responding to a hand signal and word. You can leave it like this, but if you want to teach him to respond to the word alone, reduce the hand signal gradually until he no longer needs it to complete the exercise.

9. Progress until you can say the word and the dog will repeat the action without needing to follow your hand. This is when he is beginning to listen to your word and to understand what it is that you want him to do.

5. **As soon as your dog does as you want, reward him with food and fuss.** Well done!

6. **At this stage, do not give your dog any words of command.** If you repeat "sit" when your dog is confused, he will not understand.

7. **Repeat several times, until your dog is doing the action reliably. Then begin to say your word as the dog is doing the action.** What word will you use? If you decide upon the word "sit" no one should tell your dog to "sit down" as this then becomes confusing.

10. Start varying the rewards. Use a different or less interesting reward sometimes.

11. Gradually vary and decrease the rewards given. Rewards should now come on a random basis.

12. Repeat this sequence in different places with an increasing number of distractions.
Practice in different parts of the house, in the yard, on walks, on different surfaces, when you are sitting or standing up, in the company of other people, and even in the company of other dogs.

5. down

Some dogs find this exercise easy, others find it comparatively difficult.

Make sure that your dog understands the "sit" word first. If you try to teach too much at once, he will simply become confused and not know what you are asking him.

The aim is to teach your dog to lie down on the floor when you ask him to.

Follow the procedure already outlined.
• Get your dog's attention. Get him to sit, and reward him for doing this.
• Show him another treat.
• Put it near the end of his nose.
• Slowly move the treat downwards, to a spot between his paws.
• Wait for a few moments. Provided they are interested in the treat, many dogs will lie down just to keep a close eye on it. Reward immediately.
• If he stands up, start again. Once he learns that he gets no reward for this response, he will stop doing it.
• If he seems to be losing interest, you may need to follow a process known as "shaping."

SHAPING means that instead of waiting for the end result before rewarding, you reward any steps towards the desired result.

• If your dog does not lie down quickly, make it easier for him to understand what you want.

Be patient and lure your dog into the position. Do not push or force him as this will make learning much slower. Remember, he should want to do things for you.

• Have a few treats in your hand so that you can reward him several times without breaking off.

• Show him the treat. Begin to move your hand downwards. If his head follows at all, reward him for dropping his head.

• Produce another treat; this time, if he will follow the treat to the floor, reward this.

• Next time, move the treat to the floor and wait for a few seconds. If your dog follows this with his head, reward him. If he shows any signs of moving his front feet to lie down, reward this.

• It does not matter how many stages you go through until your dog understands what you want. Be patient. Each time, you must ask for a little more from your dog before he gets the reward.

Once he is lying down by following the treat, begin to think about the word you will use.

If "down" means "lie down," make sure no one says "down" meaning don't jump up, get off the furniture, or come downstairs. Maybe use a word such as "off" for this. If you know that you say "down," meaning "don't jump up," it may be easier to teach your dog a different word for "lie down" such as "flat" or "lie."

Follow the procedure. If your dog has some difficulty doing these, do not be surprised. Dogs learn according to the situation. This is why it is essential to teach in all different circumstances. Do not assume that your dog will generalize the meaning of the word unless you have taught him in that setting.

For Experts

As with the sit, does your dog understand the word in different contexts: for example if he is in a different position, if you are not looking at him, or if you are lying on the sofa?

6. stand and roll over

1. Teaching a stand

This is something that you may or may not want. The difficulty is that dogs are more likely to move from standing than they are from sitting or lying down, so it is of less practical use.

It would be taught in exactly the same way. Lure your dog into a standing position using the treat. Keep the treat still or the dog will move to follow it.

Reward before your dog moves at all. Gradually increase the time he has to stand.

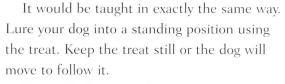

Grooming is much easier if your dog is cooperating with you and understands what you want.

2. Teaching a dog to stand still when being handled

This is extremely useful and something that I feel all dogs should be taught. However, it is separate from the exercise just described.

A dog should be happy to accept being handled but without a word being used. The dog can move slightly but should stay still enough to enable you or the veterinarian to handle, brush, dry, or examine him with relative ease and without the dog becoming anxious.

3. Roll over

Roll over as a trick:

There is more on teaching tricks later, but this is an easy, fun thing to teach your dog.

When the dog is happy to lie down on command, get him to lie down on a reasonably comfortable floor. A dog will be more willing to lie down on warm rug, than on cold concrete.

Reward him for this.

Show him the treat and move it in such a way that the dog rolls onto his side. Reward him for doing this.

Using the shaping technique, gradually teach him to roll further and further to get the treat until he is happy and able to roll right over onto his other side.

Take care:

• Slender dogs with thin coats, such as greyhound types, will find this uncomfortable unless you provide a soft floor.
• Do not reward your dog with a treat when he is lying on his back, since there is a danger of him choking. Use another reward or signal, such as the clicker or verbal praise, and give him the treat when he is the right way up again.

Teaching the dog to allow himself to be rolled over:
There will be times when your dog needs to be rolled over to allow for examination of his stomach, or perhaps for grooming. It is easier to teach your dog to let himself be rolled over by you when he is calm. Practice in different situations. This way, when you do need to do it for real, such as if your dog has had an accident or is with the vet, he will be less anxious about it.

Teach this gradually. Many dogs find it very worrying when their owner tries to roll them over. Choose a time when your dog is calm and relaxed but not fast asleep. Gradually begin shaping his behavior. If he resists, do not struggle with him, since this will make things worse; simply take your time and aim for gradual improvement. When stroking your dog, try to manoeuver him gently toward rolling over, in a relaxed way.

If your dog is not at all happy with this, stop and seek advice from a vet, trainer, or behavior consultant.

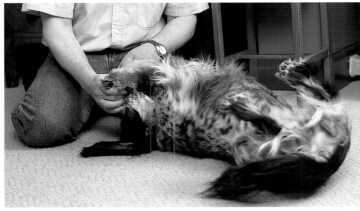

Teach this trick gradually, and learn from your own dog. Relaxed, confident young dogs tend to learn this most quickly. If your dog is apprehensive or nervous, either of you or anything in his surroundings, he will probably be reluctant to put himself in this vulnerable position. If this is the case, resolve the existing difficulties before teaching this trick.

7. stay

Once your dog has learned the words to move into the sitting and lying down positions, you can progress. It is great to have a dog who sits when told, but not so good if he leaps to his feet immediately. Therefore, we need a word that means "do not move for now." This is when we teach the stay exercise.

• When you have your dog's attention, ask him to sit and show him the treat. Instead of giving it to him immediately, wait for a moment.
• If he moves, simply start again.
• If he stays still for one or two seconds (no more!) reward him for this and encourage him to move.
• Repeat, gradually lengthening the time.
• What word will you use? If "stay" means "do not move from that position, I will reward you for being there," do not confuse him, for example do not say "stay" when you are going out of the door and leaving him. The word must be a contract, "do not move, I will come back and reward you for being there."
• When you feel he is ready for you to introduce the word, say this as soon as he is sitting.

• Get your dog to sit.
• Say "stay."
• After one or two seconds, reward him with the click, if using, the food and a fuss.
• Say your release word and encourage your dog to move. He does not need another treat for this.

Aim for gradual progress, as your dog increases in his understanding. Do not try to walk away from your dog in the early stages.

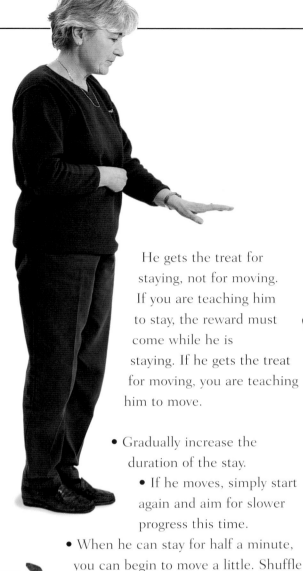

He gets the treat for staying, not for moving. If you are teaching him to stay, the reward must come while he is staying. If he gets the treat for moving, you are teaching him to move.

• Gradually increase the duration of the stay.
    • If he moves, simply start again and aim for slower progress this time.
• When he can stay for half a minute, you can begin to move a little. Shuffle your feet at first. Then reward him for staying still.
    • Soon you will find that you can take one pace away before returning to him and rewarding him.
        • Do not aim to progress too quickly.

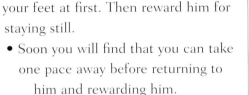

• As your dog learns to stay for increasing lengths of time, make sure that you can come back to him, reward him calmly and leave him again without him moving. This way he learns that when you say "stay," all he has to do is sit there and wait for the good things to come to him. The release word should be a slight disappointment to him, since it tells him the good things have finished for the time being.

The down stay is taught in exactly the same way as the stand stay.

By teaching the stay exercises, your dog learns to listen to you and to respond to you, even if he would prefer to be doing something else. It is a great way for building control over your dog and helping to calm a young, excitable or boisterous dog.

Other Points

Using a Release Word

If you have a word that means "do not move," you must also have a word that means "okay, now you can move." This is called a release word. Decide what you want to use. It may be "OK," or "off you go." It is not a good idea to use "good dog" or anything similar as a release word. Praise should always be used, but it does not mean that you want your dog to move. It should mean "well done, carry on." Keep praise separate from your release word.

8. wait

Another exercise, called "wait," is similar but far more practical than the "stay."

The aim is to teach your dog that "wait" means "hold on for a moment."

The release word then follows, meaning "OK, now you can get what you want."

This word can be used:
- before the dog is fed
- before he goes through a doorway
- before his leash is removed
- before you let him out of the car
- on walks, if he is pulling on his leash
- when your dog is excited, since it is a good way of getting him to stop and listen to you.

Even very young puppies can enjoy learning the basics.

It is a good way of stopping your dog for a moment and regaining control.

The first stage involves using a treat.

Sit or kneel on the floor. Have your dog on one side of you. Hold his leash or collar.

Have a treat in your other hand. Put it on the floor but prevent your dog from getting it by holding him or by picking up the treat again.

When he is not struggling to get it, let him go forward and encourage him to eat it.

Begin to introduce the words.

Hold your dog, put the treat on the floor and say "wait."

It is vital that your dog does not get the food, otherwise he will learn that "wait" signals a great game where he grabs any food he can.

Hold your dog or pick the food up again if he is trying to reach it.

As soon as he is not pulling towards the food, say your release word and, if necessary, encourage him to eat the food by pointing to it, or moving it.

The rules are the same.

"Wait" means "hold on." You must make sure that the dog does not move and get the reward.

As soon as your dog stops pulling forward, you can reward him by giving your release word.

The reward to your dog will be doing what he wanted, for example getting out of the car, going off his leash, or going through the doorway.

It does not matter what words you use, provided everyone is consistent. Use whatever words suit you. You could teach your dog to stay when you say "bananas" and to wait when you say "apples." It would not matter to the dog, but we as owners would find it much harder. Therefore, decide on the word you prefer, write it on your dog dictionary sheet, and keep to the same word.

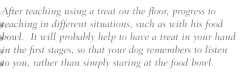

After teaching using a treat on the floor, progress to teaching in different situations, such as with his food bowl. It will probably help to have a treat in your hand in the first stages, so that your dog remembers to listen to you, rather than simply staring at the food bowl.

Repeat in different situations. Make sure that your hand movements are not giving your dog more cues than your voice. Therefore, be aware, if you point at the food, that you must release your grip on your dog's collar, for example. Even when your dog can do this with a piece of food, it does not mean that he will know what you mean when you do not want him to jump out of the car. Remember situational learning? You must teach in every different set of circumstances.

9. catch

While not exactly an exercise, teaching your dog to catch is a great way of improving his responsiveness to you, helping you to get his attention, as well as being fun to teach.

Decide what you are going to use. Treats are a great idea. A toy can also be used as long as your dog is keen on it. The problem with a toy is that you then have to take it away from your dog again. Do not throw anything that you feel may be too small and would cause your dog to choke.

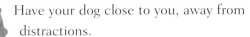

As with all exercises, you must be able to get your dog to look at you and your dog must want to learn. Many dogs find this exercise great fun once they can be successful, so it can be a wonderful way to motivate.

Have your dog close to you, away from distractions.

Get your dog's attention and show him the treat (or toy). Make sure that he can concentrate on it for a few seconds.

Throw it in the air, so that it will come down as near to your dog's mouth as possible.

Some dogs are natural at this and will catch it on the first attempt. Praise this and tell him how wonderful he is. This can then be used whenever you need to keep your dog focused on you. He cannot catch the treat if he is not watching you. He does not know when the treat will leave your hand, so he has to concentrate on you.

However, some dogs do not get the hang of this game so quickly and may need some practice.

If you throw the treat and your dog makes an effort to catch it, praise this, let the dog get the treat from the floor, and practice.

If your dog makes no attempt to catch the treat:
• Make sure that he can see it. Dogs with hair over their eyes may find this game more difficult. Consider cutting or tying back the hair.
• Make sure that the treat is something he really likes. He will not make an effort if the food isn't worth it.
• Make sure that your throws are good. Practice when your dog is not around if necessary.

If he is still not catching the treat, introduce a little competition element. Throw the treat and try to snatch it back from the floor before he gets it. (Do not tell him not to get it, that would defeat the purpose.)

If he feels he has to get it before you, he is likely to try to get it as quickly as possible.

Do not try this with a dog who can be aggressive over food or when there are quick movements.

If your dog enjoys this, use it when you want him to concentrate on you, or even just to calm him down a little if he is overexcited.

Some dogs find it incredibly difficult to understand. If you own one of these dogs, do not worry about it.

This is perhaps the only exercise that puppies find harder than adult dogs. This is because their coordination is not fully developed. Therefore, if your puppy finds it difficult, simply wait a few weeks before trying again.

This exercise is best taught to one dog at a time. Although competition between dogs could lead to increased motivation, it could also lead to squabbles for the food or toy.

10. no

Again, this is not so much an exercise as a basic life skill that all dogs must learn. We have discussed teaching our rules to our dog. Every dog needs to know that a certain word means "stop, that is not right."

Do not confuse this with scolding your dog. We can assume that any mistakes he makes are because he did not know what he should be doing. Therefore, how would it help to scold him? It is purely because our teaching has not been complete, which is not his fault.

Instead, the word "no" should be an educational word, meaning simply "that is not what I want."

It should be said, like all commands to our dog, in a voice loud enough for him to hear. The aim is not to shout so loud that he becomes frightened.

Starting from the first day with your new puppy or dog, teach that "no" means "stop, you cannot do this."

If he is doing something he should not, say "no" and move him away. Give him something else that he can do.

Do not shout, do not be angry. You are simply explaining the rules to him.

Whenever you say "no," be prepared to enforce this, by gently moving him if necessary. You cannot say "no" and then ignore him. If he does not stop, you must go to him and gently move him. If he does stop what he is doing, give an appropriate reward.

"No means no, end of discussion."

11. your dog's name

This is not an exercise for your dog, it is for the humans in the family. What do you mean when you say your dog's name? Many people have never given this any thought, yet it is something they repeat many times each day. What should his name mean? I would suggest it means "look at me, something wonderful is about to happen." It is the way of switching him on and saying "I am talking to you, we are going to do something nice together."

His name should not mean "no" or "stop." It must signal good things. If you associate your dog's name with something unpleasant, do not be surprised when he ignores you when you call his name. He will have learned that he does not want to listen to you.

To teach him to respond to his name, read the section on getting your dog's attention, and also teaching "catch." He should know that his name means "listen to me, since something good will happen." You can then use it before you ask him to do an exercise, so that your dog is paying attention and wanting to learn.

Other Points

Use the Right Name

Be consistent with his name, just as with all the words you expect him to respond to. Therefore, have as many pet names for your dog as you like, but when you are talking to him and want a response, use the same name each time.

Your dog should want to be with you when you say his name.

12. tricks

Teaching tricks to your dog can be great fun. They can be purely for fun, such as weaving in and out of your legs, or can serve a useful purpose, such as fetching named items for you or closing the door.

Some people feel that teaching tricks is demeaning to the dog. This depends on what is taught and how. Dogs love learning and they love being appreciated, so tricks can be a good way of doing this.

Whatever you decide to teach your dog, it is still of benefit. The more you successfully teach your dog, the more you learn about each other.

Often, teaching tricks is easy and fun. We give huge rewards as we are so pleased that our dog has learned. If we approach the conventional teaching in the same way, results may come more quickly. Therefore, think of teaching your dog to walk on a loose leash as just being another trick, and it often becomes much easier.

As you and your dog learn more from each other, you can teach tricks that are useful and help your dog to be a useful member of the family, such as bringing you the television remote control, fetching you his bowl at feeding time, collecting the mail or the newspaper, or closing the door. The list is endless and is only restricted by your imagination.

With any trick, split it into small segments and teach each one at a time. If it is a complicated sequence, start with the last element and teach this first. Then add the previous element to the beginning and build up from there. This process is known as "reverse chaining." It helps the dog to learn since he always ends with the familiar part.

Teaching a play bow is slightly more complicated, but the same principles apply. Motivate and reward your dog. The left hand is there to support the dog, not to pull or force him.

Shaping is also important. Instead of waiting for the whole result before rewarding your dog, you reward him for getting nearer and nearer to your goal. Each time, you need to ask him for a little more.

The same processes still apply for teaching each element. Find a way that your dog wants to do it and reward him for this.

Clickers can be extremely useful here since you can reward your dog at the right moment, even if he is some distance from you, for example, when jumping.

Suggested tricks include:
- give a paw
- roll over
- catch
- find members of the household or named toys
- close the door
- open a box
- fetch named objects for you

Tricks can be for fun, or may be used to teach more serious exercises. In this instance, Heidi has been taught to pass the crutch to her owner.

- empty the washing machine
- bark on command
- take a handkerchief from your pocket and give it to you when you sneeze
- weave through your legs
- jump over low objects
- jump over something, wait on the other side, and jump back over when you call
- crawl under a chair or low table
- put garbage in the trash.

Be imaginative! Think of what your dog enjoys and develop this to include a whole repertoire of tricks. We are limited only by our own imaginations.

training
classes

Although helpful for many dogs, training classes are not suitable for all dogs, and not all dogs would benefit from attending them.

Classes vary considerably. Consult other dog owners, then ring up and have a chat with a recommended instructor. If you like the sound of it, ask if you can go along and watch, without your dog.

Start early with your dog or puppy. Good habits are best established early and prevention is better than cure.

Consider the following:
• Are the dogs enjoying themselves?
• And the owners?
• And the instructor?
• Are the dogs learning what they should learn? For example, some classes encourage dogs to run free together. While many dogs and owners enjoy this, there is a high chance of dogs learning to play roughly or even to fight.
• Is the class small enough for people to be able to get individual attention when needed?

• Is the class reasonably quiet? Some noise is inevitable, but if there is a lot of barking and shouting, it may not be the best place for your dog to learn good manners.
• What are they teaching? If you own a pet dog, you need a class that is teaching exercises relevant to real life.
• Is it the type of class that you feel would benefit you and your dog?

If you feel happy with the class you have seen, enrol your dog for the next available course.

Be prepared to travel to your class. The nearest club may not be the best one.

Different types of classes that may be on offer:

Puppy classes. These are for young puppies, up to the age of approximately 16–18 weeks. Find a good class and reserve a place early. A good puppy class is of great benefit to most puppies and owners. Classes should be specifically for puppies. Small groups are important since puppies learn quickly and can pick up unwanted habits rapidly.

Petdog classes. If you own a pet dog, look for a class that teaches exercises you will find relevant, as well as helping to develop your understanding of your dog. These classes are not the place to go if you have a problem with your dog's behavior. They are not reform schools for difficult dogs but are more like a finishing school for dogs who have reached a certain standard and need to learn more. Classes should include basic manners, socializing and understanding your dog as well as learning to respond to your commands. If you are experiencing problems with your dog's behavior, which means that classes are not suitable, see the next chapter.

Other Points

Specialist Classes

These will include obedience classes, agility, and ringcraft. They are great if you want to learn more about that area of competition but may not be so relevant to normal life with your pet dog. Once you have achieved a certain standard, these could be something to try.

equipment

Whatever equipment you use with your dog, check it regularly. Check:

• for wear and tear.

• that it still fits correctly. This is especially important with growing puppies.

• for signs of chewing, which could weaken it.

Essential equipment for all dogs:

• A **normal collar** with either a buckle or clip. It should not have any tightening action, such as a choke or halfcheck chain.

• A **leash.** A leash of 4–6 feet is ideal. If it is shorter than this, you may find that your dog will pull more, since he cannot get away from the tight feeling.

If it is longer, it can be difficult to control your dog. Most people prefer nylon, leather, or canvas leashes. Chain can be used, but this can be very uncomfortable.

• Some form of **poop scoop** is also essential each time you take your dog out.

Alternative equipment:

Headcollars work on a similar principle to a horse's headcollar, in that they control the head. They are extremely useful with dogs that pull, jump up at passersby and are more difficult to control. It will not teach your dog how to behave, but it will make it easier to control him while you are teaching. Many dogs are not impressed at first and may scratch and shake their heads. Take your time and introduce it gradually, following the manufacturer's guidelines.

Some harnesses have been specially developed to help while teaching a dog not to pull. Be aware of what is available and use what is most suitable for you and your dog.

Harnesses are favored by many people when walking their dogs. It means that if the dog does pull, it will not hurt his neck. However, many dogs can pull more strongly with a harness, and dogs who are required to pull, for example sled dogs and tracking dogs, would wear a harness for this purpose.

For dogs who pull, there are relatively new types of harness available. They are designed to help while teaching a dog not to pull. They work by putting pressure in a different place when the dog pulls, and therefore he cannot lean into it as he does with a collar.

An extending or retractable leash consists of a box which you hold, with a line that extends as your dog pulls. There is a brake to stop. These are useful when you are in a situation where your dog can have more freedom, but cannot safely be off his leash. Please be careful—if they are used near traffic, dogs can still be involved in accidents.

A long line, or old clothesline, can be useful when your dog can have some freedom but is not safe off the leash, or when teaching a dog to come when called. Some people find it difficult to use as the excess leash can get tangled. Take care with big or strong dogs—consider wearing gloves to avoid rope burn on your hands. It may be beneficial to use under guidance from an experienced trainer.

Poopscoop, plastic bag, etc. Never leave home without these. Even if you don't need them for your dog, you may be able to donate one to another owner!

Headcollars can be a great help with dogs who are strong or boisterous. They can make walking more pleasant for all concerned.

games

We have looked at the importance of playing, controlling the games and teaching rules, as well as the pros and cons of different games. Here are some games that help the dog to use his brain and develop his senses rather than just exercise his body. By playing these challenging games, your dog will be learning to listen to you, to concentrate, and to improve his memory.

These games can be played in the house, in the yard, on walks, in fact anywhere!

Suggestions for games

• Hide a toy or treat in the house or outside. Ask your dog to find it. You may need to help him a little.

While you hide the toy, either move the dog so that he is out of sight or pretend to place the toy in several different places.

Dogs love to sniff so turn it into a constructive game.

While it is essential that games are fun, it is important to have some degree of control over your dog.

• Throw the toy into grass so that it is not visible. Send him to find it. *Make the game more difficult by:*
• Not sending your dog for a minute or so, so that he is less likely to remember the exact place.
• Calling your dog away from the toy and then sending him to find it.
• Calling your dog away, then doing something else, like asking him to sit or even fetch another toy, before sending him out to find the first toy.

• Inside the house, have a selection of boxes. They can be cardboard or perhaps empty (clean) margarine or icecream cartons. Hide a toy or treat under one. Either have your dog out of the room or, if he is watching, pretend to hide it under each. Send your dog to find it.

He may knock the boxes over to get it, or he may prefer to indicate it by pawing at it. You can then lift it for him to gain his reward.

This game can be made more difficult as detailed above.

• On a walk, drop a toy or treat on to the grass as you walk. Stop after one or two paces and call your dog to you. Send him to find his reward.

As he progresses with this game, you can take more steps away from it before calling your dog and sending him to find it.

A game involving trying to catch the dog may be fun at the time, but becomes frustrating and annoying when the dog plays it in different circumstances. Always be aware of what your dog is learning from his game.

• Throw a toy away from your dog, but hold onto him. Then send him to get it.

Make this game harder by throwing the toy and calling your dog away from it first, then sending him for it.

• Develop the game by throwing two toys in different directions and asking your dog to get one first, come back to you and then get the second. Let him choose which he collects first.

• Teach your dog to collect a named toy.

• Throw out two toys and send him for one specific toy. He should bring this to you before you send him back for the second toy.

• Make this game harder by throwing two toys, sending him for one, taking it from him, throwing it again, and letting him get this before sending him for the second toy.

• On walks, use naturally occurring obstacles to add interest to the walk. This could involve jumping fallen tree trunks, negotiating streams, jumping on and off a low wall.

• When throwing a toy for your dog, do not always throw it in the direction he is expecting. If he runs in one direction in anticipation, throw it in the opposite direction, or call him back to you before you throw it. When playing these games, stand in the middle of the field so that you can throw in any direction. In the house, stand in the hallway by an open door, so that you have several directions which you can throw in.

• This game is particularly good for dogs who love to chase. It enables the dog to learn the rules of the game, so that even when the dog is chasing something, if the owner calls, he should go back to him.

Have two toys, a favorite and a less preferred toy. You will also need either another person to help or your dog on a long leash.

Stand in the middle of the room, yard, or field. Throw the less preferred toy for the dog to fetch. Repeat this game a few times.

Then, throw the less preferred toy in such a way that your dog will run after it, even though you are not saying "fetch." Stop your dog from getting the toy—either your helper catches the toy and holds it so the dog cannot get it, or you hold the line yourself to prevent the dog from reaching the toy.

Practise playing catch with your dog in a larger area, such as a field, and get him to run further to fetch the toy.

Fun games can be played when your dog is on a leash.

Call your dog to you. Most dogs will not respond immediately, but once they realize they cannot have the toy, they will turn to look at you. As he looks at you, praise him, and produce the favorite toy. Throw this toy behind you, allow the dog to fetch it, and repeat the exercise.

The idea is to teach the dog that if he is chasing something and you call him, he should come to you since you have something even better for him, and you are more interesting than the thing is he chasing.

• Encourage your dog to work for part of his daily portion of food. If he is fed on a dried food, scatter it around the house or yard. If you feed a wet food, divide it into portions and place in small bowls or margarine lids. Then ask your dog to find the food. Make sure that you remove uneaten food afterwards.

• Even when your dog is on a leash, you can get him to catch appropriate toys or treats, or look for treats you drop, or you can run with him or play controlled tug games. All of these help to make life more interesting.

tips
for happy playing

Make walks interesting for your dog.

Make sure your dog is always successful. If he is successful, he will be rewarded and enjoy playing games with you. Make it easy at first. Gradually increase the difficulty as your dog becomes more skillful.

Give the minimum intervention necessary to be sure success. If you need to help, resist the urge to do it for him but simply help and encourage. For example, if he is hunting for a toy in long grass, do not point to it, but keep telling him to find it in different areas, gradually getting closer to the toy. Then he can find it himself.

Your dog must be motivated to find the toy or treat that you have thrown or hidden. There is no point playing these games if your dog is not interested in the reward. We are asking him to put a lot of mental effort into this, so it must be worth his while to do so.

By playing the right games, you can exercise and control your dog on walks. It should be fun and rewarding for both of you.

Equally, make sure that there are no distractions during the early stages. Many dogs love these games and will ignore other dogs or people in order to play, but in the first stages, play away from distractions.

Do not try to control your dog too closely. If you are hiding a treat, either shut him away, fasten him up, or get someone to hold him. Only make him sit and stay if he is already extremely good at this exercise. If you are telling him to sit and stay repeatedly, not only will it spoil your training, but it can quickly make the game lose its appeal.

Some of these games are easier if they are initially taught when the dog is on his leash. This way, you can make sure that he does not "cheat," and, if you are outside, he will not wander away if he gets distracted.

Make sure the game is fun. These games involve controlling your dog quite closely, so they are great for developing control. However, if you find that your dog is not interested, use less control and only begin to introduce this again when he is really hooked on the games.

Know your own dog. While many of these games are suitable for the vast majority of dogs, be aware of what suits your dog. For example, an older dog should not be hurtling around the woods. Take care if you own a dog who is possessive about food when playing games for treats. Many of these games can be adapted for dogs who have

Everyone in the family should be involved in playing with your dog, just as they are with training. However, make sure the games involving children are always supervised and are appropriate for the dog and child involved. If your dog understands the rules when playing with you, it is more likely that a child will enjoy playing with him.

disabilities or are recovering from an operation or injury and therefore need limited exercise, but check with your vet if you are unsure. As with most things, the more you put in with your dog, the more you will gain. These games involve owner concentration; they cannot be played while you are doing something else. However, most dogs will love these games, and if you take the time to teach them to your dog, you will have far greater control over him.

common behavior
problems

4

What is a behavior problem?

A behavior problem is when a dog is acting in a way that the owners wish he would not. These range from minor, which most people choose to live with, to severe, where the pleasures of living with the dog are affected by the problem behavior. This is when people usually decide they must do something about it.

Behavior that is a problem for one family may not be perceived as a problem for another. Therefore, if your dog is behaving in a way that you do not find acceptable, that is the time to take steps.

When a dog behaves in a way that we do not want or expect, many people give labels such as "naughty," "disobedient," or "spiteful," when really the dog is usually behaving in a normal way, behaving as he has been taught or is simply confused.

problem behavior
possible causes

Normal behavior. This is when a dog is behaving in a normal, canine way but at an inappropriate time or place, or to an inappropriate extent. The dog usually has his own reasons for doing this and often finds it rewarding.

Most "problem" behavior is only a problem for us, not for our dog.

Examples include:

It is normal to bark, but it is a problem for most people if the dog barks at every noise or movement and continues to bark.

Dogs need to empty their bladders regularly, but if your dog repeatedly chooses to do this on your bed, you have quite a different problem.

Dogs use aggression when they feel it necessary to resolve a situation. However, if the dog is showing aggression to the owner, it is not acceptable.

Learned behavior. This is where the dog has been taught to behave in a certain way, usually without the owner being aware.

Confusion. Owners can appear inconsistent to dogs. Maybe we allow them to jump up one day, but shout the next because we have work clothes on. Maybe we allow them on the sofa when we are watching TV, but not the next evening when visitors arrive. One day they are rewarded by a fuss when they pester for attention, the next day they are shouted at since we have other things on our minds. We allow them privileges but expect them to do as they are told. We expect our dogs to understand all of this but frequently they have no idea of what we want. Inconsistent, aggressive, overactive behavior can result.

Abnormal, maladaptive behavior. This is less common. It is where the dog is not acting in his best interests and his behavior affects his quality of life. Examples include some phobias, selfmutilation, stereotyped behavior, and some obsessive behavior.

Special circumstances. It may be that the dog's behavior is not normally a problem, but special circumstances

Case history

Misty

Mrs. Smith was apprehensive of large dogs. When walking her spaniel she would hurriedly walk away from any dogs approaching and would not allow Misty to go anywhere near them. Misty learned that her owner did not like other dogs and began growling at them in an attempt to keep them away. This made Mrs. Smith keep her distance even more, and Misty became increasingly aggressive at the sight of another dog. Mrs. Smith was convinced that the other dogs had frightened Misty and had no idea that she had created this behavior.

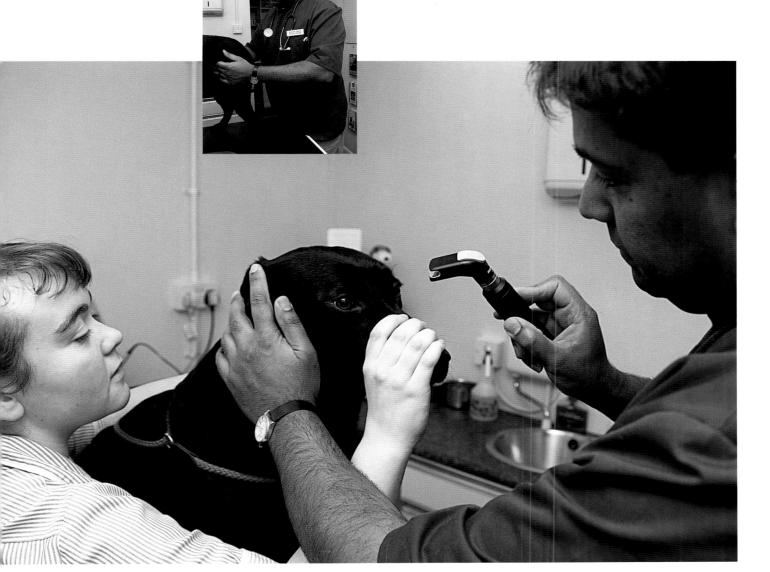

A visit to the veterinary surgeon should be the first step in identifying and treating a behavior problem. A thorough check up and chat with the vet should help in deciding what steps to take next.

within the family mean that it is no longer acceptable and something must be done about it.

Example: Ben had always pulled on his leash, but Tony, the teenage son, had enjoyed and encouraged this. However, when Tony left home, his mother found she could no longer manage to walk Ben on her own because he was too strong and she felt she would be pulled over.

Physical problems. Sometimes a dog can have a physical problem that appears to be a behavior problem. This is why a thorough checkup by a veterinarian is vital.

Example: A dog with a skin allergy may be more irritable or active than normal because of discomfort. A dog with a bladder infection may appear to have a house-breaking problem, but the behavior is not under his control.

general **principles**

There are basic principles to apply, whatever behavior you are attempting to modify or avoid.

Reward good behavior. At all times, reward good behavior. A reward is anything that a dog wants at the time, so use whatever is appropriate.

Although we may be trying to help, some methods can make a situation worse. For example, trying to force a nervous dog forward will make him feel more apprehensive.

Teach yourself to notice good behavior. It is all too easy to take good behavior for granted and only notice misbehavior, but this can worsen the situation. Whenever your dog does something good, give an appropriate reward.

Example: Sparky was "always on the go." Then his owner started to notice every time he relaxed and lay down. "Good boy," she said with a smile, occasionally going to him to fuss him. Sparky began to lie down more often as it brought him attention.

A behavior which brings a reward will be repeated.

Example: Penny was overenthusiastic with visitors, so Jeanette asked her visitors to ignore Penny for jumping up but to make a huge fuss of her when she sat. Treats were also used to encourage sitting and to provide a better reward. Penny had no need to jump up since sitting brought her much better results.

Ignore unwanted behavior. Getting angry and issuing threats and punishment can hinder progress, so it may often be best to control the situation by ignoring any unwanted behavior.

Example: Sam barked and lunged at other dogs. He would bark and leap around and his owner would then shout and pull on the leash. To Sam's mind, she was simply joining in, so Sam continued. Lyn then decided just to move Sam away from other dogs, since shouting was obviously not stopping him. She could then reward him for being quiet. Although this did not cure Sam's behavior completely, it did help the situation.

Example: Barney loved attention and learned to pick up papers out of the bin as someone would then chase him to get them back. As soon as his owners stopped playing this game, and ignored the misbehavior, Barney learned that there was no point in repeating it because there would be no reaction, and stopped doing it.

Do not give unwanted signals. If we are worried about how our dog is going to behave, we tend to alter our behavior. While it is essential to ensure safety, it is important not to give the dog extra triggers for unwanted behavior with our own behavior.

For many dogs, any attention is better than nothing and therefore, they will repeat undesirable habits in the hope of getting some reaction. To stop the habit, ignore rather than chastize.

Example: Because Sheeba was likely to lunge at people on the street, Mrs. Roberts would tighten her lead when she saw anyone approaching. Sheeba learned that a tight lead was the signal to begin barking and jumping.

Example: Michelle was keen that Jo-jo would get on with her young nephew but was worried in case things went wrong. Whenever they were together, Michelle would become tense and anxious and subconsciously hold her breath. Jo-jo sensed his owner was not her usual self and became anxious himself whenever the nephew was around. Without meaning to, Michelle had fulfilled her own worst fear.

Always be aware of what you are doing and do not give extra cues to your dog.

Do not reward unwanted behavior. Make sure that you are not rewarding the very behavior you want to stop. Watch yourself, or ask someone else to observe, to make sure that you are not teaching the wrong things.

Example: Harry would go berserk, whenever the mailman arrived. Mrs. Jones would take him by the collar and lead him away. "Good boy, it's all right, he's gone now, good boy," she would say in her attempts to calm him down. Harry heard "Good boy" and assumed Mrs. Jones was rewarding his behavior.

Example: Flossie loved her owner's attention but hated fireworks. Any strange bangs would have her trembling and shaking. Mr. Richards would then take her onto his knee and cuddle her, telling her what a good girl she was. Although Flossie's fear was real, she learned that her best times were when she was afraid since she loved the cuddles, so she began to become increasingly fearful for less reason.

If you do not want your dog to jump up at people, do not play games where he is rewarded for jumping at you.

Life Skills

Safety is Essential

Control measures may include:
• keeping your dog on a leash on walks if he is not reliable.
• putting a muzzle on your dog at the vet's if you know he is not good at being handled.
• keeping away from TV repairers if your dog does not like workers in the house.
• taking your dog away from a situation if you are not confident with him.
Safety must always come first.

Avoid aggression. As a species, we are quick to resort to aggression. When our dogs misbehave, some display of aggression from humans often follows. However, trying to hurt, frighten, or intimidate our dogs is rarely effective. It can make the situation worse. The old approach of "show him who's boss," meaning to resort to something physical, has fortunately been replaced with more understanding and effective methods. It is not possible to overcome aggression with aggression. All the dog will learn is that whoever is most aggressive will win. He may back down this time, but the problem is likely to show itself in a worse form sooner or later.

Example: Samson growled at his owner when he was scolded for coming into the house with muddy paws. "I'll teach you to growl," roared Brian, hitting the dog hard. Samson growled again, in self-defense, and Brian, convinced the dog was defying him, lost his temper. He wasn't bitten on that occasion, but Samson lost trust in his owner and avoided him when possible.

When meeting other dogs, a tight leash can inadvertently become the signal for aggression.

Avoid practice at problem behavior. It is sensible to make sure that your dog does not have the opportunity to practice this behavior. Therefore, if your dog runs aggressively at other dogs when off his leash, it is sensible to keep him on his leash when there could be other dogs around. This will not cure the problem, and can create others, but it is important while you work on resolving the particular problem in hand.

Example: Bess would not come in from the yard when David called her. He decided that, in the short term, she would only have access to the yard when he took her out on the leash.

approaches

There are various approaches to canine behavioral problems that we can take, including:

1. Live with the problem. Many people do this. If the problem is minor and not affecting either you, the dog, or other people, it may be easier to live with it than to invest effort to resolve it.

2. Control. This approach means that you must always be one step ahead of your dog. It can be effective if you never make a mistake. However, be aware of what your dog is learning, as the problem behavior could be worsening.

Example: Jackie's dog Poppy did not like visitors. Jackie found it easier simply to keep Poppy out of the way when people came. It seemed to work in the short term, but Poppy's behavior became increasingly antisocial. On the one occasion when the door was not closed properly, Poppy ran in and bit Jackie's friend. Jackie found that because she had been shut away, Poppy was more likely to bark at people, and would not let anyone near her.

3. Training. This means teaching your dog to do something different.

Train your dog to sit and stay in a specific place—that way he will not be able to bark at visitors. Similarly, you can teach him to do a down stay, so that he cannot lunge at another dog. But remember that although these things can certainly help, there may be difficulties. Often, the dog's motivation to misbehave is far stronger than the motivation to obey. Ignoring this behavior may also be incompatible with a dog's natural instincts. For example, the dog who barks at other dogs may be afraid and so to lie down would be very stressful for him.

4. Behavior. This approach looks at why a dog is misbehaving and what can be done to make him want to do the right thing.

For example, a dog will not try to keep visitors away if he finds it is in his best interests for them to arrive because they bring him food treats or play games with him. Therefore he has no reason to be territorial or unfriendly to visitors.

Teaching the right habits is essential.

A dog showing antisocial behavior is easy to identify. Knowing how to resolve the problem and investing the hard work required is more difficult and usually involves specialist help and support.

When working with your dog it is important to:

1. Know your own dog. What is right for one dog may not be ideal for another. Adapt accordingly.

2. Assess progress. You may feel you are teaching one thing, but what is your dog learning? Make sure that you are making the progress you should expect.

3. Do not expect instant results. Most behavior problems have been developing over months or years, so will take hard work and dedication to overcome.

4. Involvement of the whole family. It is essential that everyone who is involved with the dog is consistent and follows the same rules.

5. Take advice. See later section on referral.

Resolving a behavior problem usually involves changing the way dog and owner behave and how they relate to one another.

5. Combination approach. This is probably the most effective and practical. If a dog is barking aggressively at visitors, methods of control are essential in the short term. Improved response to owners" commands will help, along with teaching the dog to want people to visit in controlled situations. This, and the realization that we may always need to take care with this dog in these circumstances, will result in a situation where everyone is happy. The appropriate cure will vary for each dog.

a closer look at:
1. trying to lead the pack

We looked at how a dog sees the pack in a previous chapter. Dogs see things differently than we do and it is important to be aware of this. Our attempts to make the dog feel happy and loved can result in him feeling insecure or having ideas of grandeur! It is essential that our dogs understand that good things come when we decide and not when *they* demand them.

Some dogs are not interested in becoming pack leaders. With these dogs, we can give the signs of not being a pack leader and there are no difficulties. However, difficulties can arise with dogs who do want to be pack leaders. These could include:

• pushy, opportunistic dogs who want to lead the pack. In the absence of a human leader, they will be only too pleased to take over and become demanding and even more pushy towards the family.

• nervous, easily excitable dogs. If they have no one to follow, they can become more anxious, feeling that they cannot rely on anyone to protect them.

Case History

Jamie

Jamie was a determined dog. In his mind, life revolved around him and he made the decisions. If he wanted something, he pestered until he got it. If he did not want something, he simply ignored his owner. One day, his owner was attempting to remove an empty crisp packet from Jamie's mouth. Jamie growled. His owner shouted. Jamie snapped, his owner hit him hard, shouting, "I'll show you who's boss!" Jamie's fighting spirit rose and he lunged at his owner, biting him hard on the hand, before he had the opportunity to hit again. His owner was puzzled. "Why did he do that?" he wondered. Jamie was also puzzled. How could his owner act like a submissive dog for most of the time, but then suddenly become aggressive for no reason?

The types of behavior shown by dogs who feel they are at the top of the pack will vary considerably, ranging from no signs at all, through ignoring the owners and displaying antisocial behavior, to severe aggression for what may appear to be no reason. This behavior is seen in both male and female dogs.

Puppies learn about pack behavior when very young. In the litter they practice different roles and skills which are put into effect as they grow older.

Is this dog sleeping or learning?

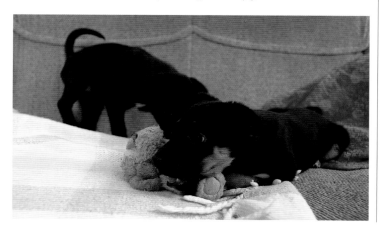

Possible causes
- Genetics play a part. Some breeds are naturally more opportunistic and forceful than others.
- Learning in the litter. Within each litter, certain dogs will be more suited to being "leader types."
- Owner behavior. How the owner treats the dog makes a huge difference.

Prevention
- Read the previous section and follow the relevant points.
- Be consistent.
- Give your dog plenty of opportunity for mental and physical stimulation.
- Training is important since it teaches a dog to enjoy responding to his owner.
- Rewarding good behavior is essential.
- Make sure that all family members are consistent.
- Make sure that your dog earns all good things.

What to do if problems have arisen
- Avoid aggression.
- Avoid confrontations and difficult situations.
- Walk away from your dog if you feel he may bite. This is not giving in to him but is simply defusing the situation and not letting him manipulate you.
- Seek expert help.

This problem is especially seen in:
- pushy, opportunistic dogs
- clever dogs
- dogs who feel their owner is not giving the right signals

Attempts to get his own way vary from subtle attention-seeking to overt aggression. Always try to see the situation from your dog's point of view.

a closer look at:
2. problems when left alone

Many dogs show unwanted behavior when left alone. Apart from cats, they are the only animal that we allow free access in our homes without supervision and expect them not to break any of our rules.

Unwanted behavior can include:
- barking, whining, howling
- chewing, scratching
- lapses in housebreaking.

Possible causes
- Anxiety about being left.
- Boredom.
- Never having been taught how to behave when left.
- Overattachment to owner.

Prevention:

We take it for granted that our dog will enjoy our company, but how many of us take time to teach him how to cope when left?

• Teach the dog to be left. Practice closing a door between you and your dog for short periods of time, when your dog is calm and settled. Return to your dog as a reward for good behavior, i.e. not barking or scratching.
Include this in normal routine. Make sure that your dog spends some time each day alone. This is essential for dogs who are not left every day.

• Give the dog plenty of things to do, with or without you. Walks and games help to tire a dog, and things to chew occupy him when you are not there.
• Ignore your dog at times. If your dog is used to having your attention at any time, it will be difficult for him when you are away. Ignore him at times during each day.
• Do not leave a dog alone for long periods. It is unfair to leave a dog alone for longer than he can cope. Consider asking neighbors or friends to stop by, or find a reputable dog walker.

What to do if problems have arisen
• Follow the above points.
• Do not get angry with your dog on your return—he does not look guilty. Owners tend to interpret their dog's look of fear as guilt that "he knows he's done wrong," and the owner feels more frustrated. Dogs do not have a sense of guilt, they are simply afraid of your reaction. Although it is difficult, do not scold your dog. It will only make matters worse. If you had a dog who was chewing because he was

---

Case History

Bertie

Bertie came from a rescue kennels. His owner loved him immediately and felt flattered when he followed her everywhere. "I can't even go to the bathroom without him," Mrs. Evans laughed. But when she went shopping a week later, she returned to devastation. Bertie had demolished the quilt. After a phone call to the local rescue, Mrs. Evans found that Bertie had had five homes and been returned each time because of destructive problems. Mrs. Evans was determined to keep Bertie and asked her vet for a referral to a specialist. It took several weeks of hard work, but Mrs. Evans could eventually leave Bertie for short periods, knowing he could cope and that her home would remain intact.

worried you were leaving him, he will now become anxious about you coming back as well.

• **Seek expert advice to help teach your dog how to cope without you.**

Many young dogs chew for enjoyment or for attention, but if destruction is on a large scale, it usually signifies that the dog is distressed.

This problem is especially seen in:

• rescue dogs
• labrador types
• dogs whose owners are with them for most of the time
• dogs left alone for long periods
• dogs who are especially close to their owners.

a closer look at:
3. overboisterous dogs

This may be a game to the bigger dog, but the smaller dog may not interpret it this way! Again, it is a normal behavior but not one which is acceptable.

What do we mean by "overboisterous?" Generally, owners use it to mean that their dog is more active than they would wish him to be.

Possible causes

• This can be a natural behavior. Look at what your dog was bred to do. If he is a working type, then a high level of activity is normal and to be expected.

• It can be a sign of stress or confusion. If a dog is uncertain or does not understand what you want, it is likely that he will show a higher level of activity.

Prevention

• Take care over your choice of dog. A working dog may look appealing, but do you have the time and energy necessary to look after it?

• Teach the right behavior from the beginning.

• Reward good behavior. Train yourself to notice when your dog is behaving well, including simply lying down quietly. Make sure that you give him an appropriate reward.

• Be a leader he wants to listen to.

What to do if problems have arisen

• Follow the above points.

• What was your dog bred for? What do you want from him? If the answers to these two questions are different, look at what more you can give him to satisfy his needs.

• If boisterousness occurs in certain situations only, set up those situations to teach your dog what behavior you would like. For example, if your dog jumps up at visitors, ask a group of friends to call around, one at a time. Instruct them to ignore any jumping up but to give lots of rewards (in the form of attention, treats, and games) for keeping four feet on the floor. Sitting brings even bigger rewards.

Ask each friend to leave after about ten minutes and call again immediately. This way, your dog is given clear messages about what behavior is rewarding.

• Be consistent. Make sure that all the family behaves in a similar way towards the dog.

Teaching the right behaviors and rewarding calmness can help a great deal when living with an energetic dog. Channel his mental and physical energies into acceptable outlets through games, exercise and training.

This problem is especially seen in:

• dogs bred to be active, e.g. working dogs
• dogs who are confused about what their owner wants
• dogs with owners who are unrealistic about how much exercise and stimulation their dog needs.

Case History

Paul and Jackie saw some Border Collie puppies advertised at a farm, and chose the cutest pup. Since both work, a neighbor used to come in during the day. As Jake grew up, Paul started to walk him in the morning before work, while Jackie took him out in the evening. As the days grew shorter and the weather colder, the walks gradually stopped. Paul and Jackie felt that, when they came home from work, all they wanted to do was watch television. Unfortunately, this was not enough for poor Jake. He would pester them all evening and barked at the slightest sound.

Paul and Jackie decided that they wanted to keep Jake and resolved to start walking him again twice a day. Walking in the cold and dark is not always fun, but it is the price to pay for owning a dog, especially an energetic and active one. The neighbor was happy to start coming in during the day to have a game with Jake. Life became more interesting for Jake, while Paul and Jackie became much fitter!

a closer look at:
4. aggression to visitors

We want our dogs to defend our home, alert us to strange noises, deter burglars, and yet be friendly to all our visitors. Not surprisingly, they sometimes make errors of judgement and do not always differentiate.

Territorial behavior develops as puppies mature. Therefore, if your puppy does not bark when the doorbell rings, do not think you have to teach him. You could be

Doors are not a natural concept for our dogs to understand.

encouraging undesirable behavior that is difficult to control as he grows up.

Most dogs show some degree of territorial behavior. Barking when someone comes to the door is usually seen as acceptable, provided the dog stops when we want. If we then take control of the situation and open the door, the dog should allow us to make the decisions. If we are happy with this person, so should he be.

Possible causes
• This is natural and it is often desirable, unless it is completely out of control.
• Dogs who practice the behavior and bark at passersby may feel that they are rewarded. As with all behavior that is rewarded, the behavior gets stronger.

Case History

Josh loves to be the center of attention and adores visitors. However, his owners find his reaction to the mailman difficult to live with. He throws himself at the door, barking, growling, and snatching at the mail. He continues leaping at the door until the mailman is several houses away.

What started as excitement soon became a game. Josh learned that he could bark at mailmen and make them go away more quickly! In his mind, the mailman was no longer a person, simply an intruder who must be kept away at all costs. And it worked—to this day, his home has never been broken into by a mailman!

• Dogs may have been encouraged by their owners. Owners saying "who's that?" in an excitable tone to their puppy when the doorbell rings may find that their dog develops a higher territorial response.

Prevention

• Socialize your dog. If he loves people, he has far less reason to want them to stay away.

• Make sure that the arrival of people means rewards for your dog, such as fuss, attention, treats, and games.

• When your puppy is young, carry him to meet mailmen, workpeople and so forth as they come to your door. Make sure he has good experiences.

• Do not allow your dog to bark at passersby. Remove him from his vantage point if necessary.

What to do if problems have arisen

• For safety's sake, keep him away from certain visitors. The person who has come to read your meter probably has no desire to help you train your dog.

• Seek expert help.

This problem is especially seen in:

• dogs of guarding breeds

• nervous dogs, who may want to avoid close proximity to strangers

• rescue dogs, who may have practiced this behavior in kennels

• active dogs with insufficient stimulation who find the arrival of visitors highly arousing.

Dogs should be encouraged to enjoy the company of other people, so that they do not see them as threatening or unwelcome.

a closer look at:
5. aggression to people outside

Although this can be linked to aggression towards visitors, it can bring its own problems. Whereas we generally have control over who comes into our houses, we can neither control nor predict who we will meet outside, or how they will react to us or our dog. Behavior can vary from occasional barking at certain individuals, to barking, snapping, and lunging at anyone the dog considers too close or a potential threat or problem.

Possible causes
• Nervousness is perhaps the most common. The dog feels that he has to keep strangers away. It is usually due to inadequate socialization, but can also be due to bad experiences in specific circumstances.
• Genetic factors can be influential.

Meeting a variety of people throughout life and enjoying being with them is important for dogs.

• Territorial behavior. The more time a dog spends in an area, the more territorial he can feel. Some dogs feel that the local park "belongs" to them.
• Expectations. If a dog is used to seeing no one on his walks, he may be startled when someone suddenly appears Again, this is linked to effective socialization.
• Learned behavior. The more a dog practices this response, the more likely he is to show it next time.
• Some dogs show this behavior to particular groups of people, such as men, children, people carrying bags, people with sunglasses on and so on.

Prevention
• Socialize. Make sure that your dog has good experiences with different types of people, in different circumstances.
• Reward good behavior.
• Be relaxed and friendly towards people. If your dog feels that you are tense when people approach, he will be the

Safety is essential if a problem has arisen. While a muzzle will not alter how the dog thinks and therefore will not cure the problem, it can be a good way to feel more confident while working to teach the dog new habits.

same. Try saying "hello" to people to show your dog that you are friendly and relaxed.

• Walk in different places, both quiet and busy, so that your dog learns to cope in all environments.

What to do if problems have arisen

• Do not reward unwanted behavior or scold the dog.

• Teach the dog the right way to behave.

• Make sure that you are not giving unwanted cues, such as becoming tense and tightening the leash.

• Seek expert advice.

This problem is especially seen in:

• nervous dogs

• dogs who were not well socialized as puppies

• dogs from rural areas.

a closer look at:
6. aggression to children

This can be linked to aggression to other types of people, or can be seen in dogs who are otherwise very friendly.

It can be seen:
• in the home. The dog displays unwanted behavior to the children within the family.
• with visitors to the home. The dog shows unwanted behavior to children who visit.
• outside. The dog is unhappy when walking past children.

Unwanted behavior varies but will include nervousness, attempts to get away, aggression ranging from tension and growling to attempts to bite.

Possible causes
• Nervousness.
• Lack of socialization. Children behave differently from adults and it is important that dogs learn what to expect.
• Bad experiences. Children can be rough and hurtful, whether or not they mean it.

• It could be that the dog objects to something, such as being handled more roughly around the tail, but adults know to read the signs and avoid this, whereas children are less observant.

Prevention
In the home
• Do not leave children and dogs alone together. Supervise all interactions.
• Make sure that the children play calm and controlled games with your dog, under supervision.
• Avoid rough and tumble and highly exciting chase games which can get out of control.
• If children are visiting, be even more vigilant.
• Notice any warning signs and take precautions. Do not wait for the dog to show severe aggression. Notice any

Aim to spend some quality time with your dog and children together. This enables child and dog to have fun while learning about each other.

This problem is especially seen in:

- dogs who are not familiar with children
- dogs in homes where the children are allowed to tease the dog
- dogs who have been undersocialized
- gentle, timid dogs who find children frightening.

Case History

Jack

Jack was a friendly puppy. Mrs. Johnson was pleased that he got on so well with her three children. As he grew older, they all played together and Mrs. Johnson stopped supervising the games since they played so nicely. One day, David, a neighbor's four-year-old, was visiting. Jack and the children, including David, were playing in the front room. Mrs. Johnson had popped into the kitchen. She heard a growl and bark and rushed in to find David crying hysterically. There was a graze on his cheek but nothing more serious. Later, she found out that a game was played where the children raced to pick up Jack's favorite toy. Jack had the toy in his mouth and David, with all the enthusiasm of a four-year-old, grabbed Jack's nose instead of the toy. Fortunately, no serious damage was done, but who was to blame? Jack, David, or Mrs. Johnson?

---

tension. Always take notice of a growl, and do not assume that your dog will not take it any further.

- Teach the rules to the children. They must always allow your dog his own space and peace and quiet when he wants it. They must be gentle and not tease or hurt him.
- Separate children and dogs at certain times, such as when the dog is eating or wants to sleep, or when the children are playing their own games.

Outside

- Socialize. Make sure that your dog has good experiences with children of all ages.

What to do if problems have arisen

- For safety's sake, keep your dog away from children.
- Seek advice immediately. Do not take any chances.

Even young children can enjoy training their dog using rewards, under supervision. Adults should teach the dog first and then help the child to learn.

a closer look at:
7. aggression to dogs outside

Good social behavior around other dogs is a must in today's society. Since there are more areas where dogs are banned, dog walkers tend to gather in suitable areas.

Antisocial behavior can include:

• nervousness. In extreme forms, this can result in the nervous dog running away which can encourage another dog to chase.

• overboisterous play. This varies—an appropriate game for one dog may not be acceptable for another.

• aggression in any form. This can range from growling and snarling to lunging and attacking.

Being on a leash can make a dog react more aggressively, since their natural movement is restricted. However, it is essential that dogs learn to cope with it since it is part of everyday life.

Possible causes

• Nervousness.

• Size differences. A powerful dog can hurt a more delicate dog without meaning to.

• Games that have become too rough, and the dog has learned to fight.

• Territorial behavior.

• Hierarchy disputes.

• Frustration. When a dog cannot have what he wants, frustration can lead to aggression.

Prevention

• Socializing. Learning to mix with a variety of dogs is essential for your dog.

• The owner must be the most important thing to the dog.

• Do not let your dog play rough games with another dog.

• Speak to other owners. Are they happy for your dog to run up to theirs?

• If another dog is on his leash and yours is off, do not allow your dog to overpower, threaten, or intimidate the other dog.

• Make sure that your dog understands that there are times when he can go to other dogs and times when he cannot.

• He should have good experiences with all kinds of dogs, on and off his leash.

• He should meet a range of dogs, which react to him in different ways. He should not assume that all dogs want to play, and should take the hint when another dog does not want to be involved.

• Make sure that you can call your dog back to you. You must be more important than any of the other dogs.

• Be realistic. Your dog may not love every dog he meets, but he should behave in a sociable way.

Case History

Fred

Julie thought it was great when Fred ran to every other dog in the park to play rough games. However, Julie did not notice that not all owners and dogs were so keen on these games, and she was very surprised one day when one owner shouted at her to control her dog since he was a nuisance. She then noticed that maybe these games were not appropriate since other dogs would yelp and run with their tail between their legs. She decided that she should play more games with Fred and distract him from other dogs. She found her walks became more fun and rewarding.

Rough games between two dogs can get out of hand and become aggressive.

What to do if problems have arisen:

• Safety and control are essential. Do not allow your dog to have free access to other dogs until the problem with his behavior is resolved.

• Seek expert advice.

This problem is especially seen in:

• breeds originally bred for fighting

• dogs who have had lots of opportunity to play roughly with other dogs

• small dogs who may feel that they need to do this in self-defense

• large dogs who have learned to bully

• exuberant dogs who feel their owners are uninteresting on a walk

• dogs who have not been adequately socialized when they were young.

a closer look at:
8. aggression to pets in the home

We keep pets because we choose to and we also expect that they will all get on together. However, this is not always the case.

Problem behavior toward other pets in the home generally involves aggression or nervous behavior.

Competition over important resources (e.g. food, toy, or attention) can provoke a dog to show aggression to his "rival."

Possible causes
• A personality clash. Just as with people, not all animals get on well together.
• Hierarchy dispute. Generally, the more similar dogs are in age, sex, temperament etc., the more likelihood there is of a dispute. It is most frequently seen in dogs of the same sex.
• Owner's intervention. In some instances, attempts by the owner to resolve the problem situation can actually make things worse.
• Predatory instincts. Many dogs have the instinct to chase small furry things that move quickly.
• Natural behavior.

Prevention
Dogs
• When acquiring a second dog, it is often best to choose one that is different from your first.

• Do not try to treat them equally. Dogs are pack animals, and usually develop their own hierarchy. Support this.
• Do not assume that your first dog should be the "top dog." Watch for any signals they are giving.
• Resist the temptation to intervene when the dogs are communicating with each other. The odd glare or growl is fine, as long as they are able to resolve any differences peacefully in the end.

Cats
• Take great care if you are thinking of introducing a cat or kitten to the household.
• Do not leave the dog and cat alone together until you are 100 percent confident about their relationship.
• Make sure that the more timid animal has some way of escaping from the other.

Other animals
• Do not assume that your dog will want to be friends any more than the other animal would want this.
• Make sure that the other animal is safely protected.

Case History

Penny and Tuppence

Penny and Tuppence were litter sisters. The James family knew that this could cause problems, so they were careful in how they treated them. When young, Penny was the first into everything and so they make sure that Penny was the first to have all the privileges and Tuppence had to wait. As they matured, Tuppence showed that she was the more confident of the two on walks, and Penny would hold back to let her go first. Back home, roles switched to their original hierarchy. Because they were aware of this, the James family were able to treat the dogs accordingly and dogs and family lived together peacefully and happily.

What to do if problems have arisen

Dogs

• You may have to intervene if fighting does start. Be prepared for this. Letting them sort things out together is not advisable if it reaches this stage.

• Try walking away or creating a diversion.

• If you decide to separate the dogs, remember that more owners are injured than dogs. Take care.

• Shouting and hitting will generally make the situation worse so avoid doing this.

• If necessary, separate the dogs in the short term. However, it may make the situation worse in the long term.

• Seek expert help.

Despite old wives' tales, cats and dogs can live peacefully and happily together.

Cats and other animals

• Separate to ensure safety.

• Take advice as to what can be done.

This problem is especially seen in:

• litter mates living together

• chase orientated dogs who may find it hard to live with cats and not chase them

• young, boisterous dogs

• owners who try to treat all dogs equally.

a closer look at:

9. nervousness and fear

Some degree of nervous behavior is essential for survival. However, some dogs take this to extremes and their behavior is out of proportion to the situation, even becoming so severe that the quality of life is affected.

Common fears include:
- people of certain types, such as men or children
- noises, especially fireworks, gunshot and thunder
- other dogs
- veterinary premises.

Some dogs generalize their fears and become afraid of other situations.

Behaviors shown include:
- running away to find security
- hiding, which may include scratching or digging at surfaces
- panting, excess salivation
- shaking or trembling
- loss of house-breaking
- whining or crying.

Possible causes

- Genetic factors.
- Prior learning.
- Lack of socializing and good experiences.
- Learned from owners" reaction.

Prevention

- Socialization when young helps a dog to learn how to cope with life. There is a direct link between lack of early socialization and fear behavior towards people and dogs.
- Good experiences in different circumstances.

When frightened, it is normal to try to get away. If escape is impossible, alternative behavior may be shown.

- Owners should insure safety but not react. Other than safety considerations, it is important that you give as little reaction as possible. If you feel anxious in the situation, your dog will become more anxious, since he will recognize your feelings. If you stare at your dog to see how he reacts, this can also make him worse.
- Do not reward nervous behavior. It is essential only to reward the behavior you want him to repeat. Do not show sympathy even though this is difficult.
- Reward confidence. As soon as your dog shows signs of recovering, however long this may take, reward him with attention and anything else he enjoys. This way he learns that all good things come to him as soon as he reacts normally.

What to do if problems have arisen

- Following the advice given above may be sufficient if the problem is in its early stages.

Case History

Cassie

Cassie was a happy dog—her tail wagged all the time, unless she heard a bang. If there was any suggestion of a sudden noise, however far away, Cassie ran to hide and would stay there for half an hour or more. She changed from being an outgoing friendly dog to a suspicious one, constantly waiting for the next noise. Her owners felt sorry for her and would follow her to her hiding place to sit with and cuddle her. After seeking expert advice, they understood that this was creating a bigger problem. Although it was very difficult for them, they stopped doing this. Using a tape recording to control the sounds, they managed to teach Cassie that good things happened when there were noises. It was a slow process, but Cassie is now able to cope with noises around her and is the happy dog she was before.

- If the behavior is more severe or well established, additional help will be needed. This will involve controlled exposure to frightening situations, linked with good experiences too.
- Seek specialist help.

Collie types have been selectively bred to have sensitive hearing, but this can cause difficulties in normal life.

This problem is especially seen in:

- collie types. They are frequently very sensitive, have good hearing and learn quickly.
- timid dogs
- dogs who have not been adequately socialized as puppies.
- dogs whose owners reward this behavior.

a closer look at:
10. car travel problems

Cars are an essential part of our lives, but our dogs do not always react well. Possible problems include:

• nervousness in the car
• car sickness
• overexcitement in the car, resulting in barking and jumping around
• problems being left in the car
• territorial aggression.

Prevention
• Teaching your dog the right behavior from the beginning is the most sensible thing to do. This means taking your dog for regular short journeys in the car.
• If possible, have someone else in the car to reward good behavior when it occurs.
• Treats are not such a good reward here, since this could make the dog feel travel sick.
• Rewards of attention or a special toy will be more effective in this situation.

What to do if problems have arisen
The solution will depend on what the dog is doing and why he his doing it.
• For nervousness in the car, see the previous section on nervous behavior. You must begin to make the car a great place to be.
• Car sickness is often linked with nervousness, since the dog learns to dislike the car. Some young dogs simply grow out of it, others don't. Again, make sure that the car is a good place to be and make frequent short trips. Maybe simply move the car a few yards at first and progress gradually.
• Overexcitement in the car, resulting in barking and jumping around, is one of the most common problems.

Do not only use the car when you are going somewhere exciting, take your dog on boring trips too. It may be a good idea to fasten your dog securely, perhaps using a car harness, for safety's sake. Reward good behavior. Resist the urge to shout and become angry since this will only make your dog more excited.
• For problems with being left in the car, see the previous section on teaching a dog to be left.
• Territorial aggression. The more time your dog spends in the car, the more likely he is to feel territorial about it. Therefore, control the situation and avoid parking in busy places where people will be walking by the car.
• If your dog jumps out of the car before you are ready, consider fastening him using a car safety harness. Read chapter 2 on teaching your dog to "wait."

Seek help if necessary for any car problems.

Case History

Stanley

Stanley loved the car. When Janet picked up the car keys and reached for her coat, Stanley knew he was in for fun. He would begin barking and spinning, which continued until they reached the park where the walk took place.

One day, Janet picked up the car keys as usual, but did not reach for her coat. When they finally did get into the car, the car stopped every time Stanley barked, and Janet simply sat still. When he was quiet, the car started again. This continued. For the first few days, they never even got to the park, but simply came home again and went for a walk later, without the car.

Eventually, Stanley accepted that the rules had changed. As soon as he barked, all progress stopped. In order for it to start again, he had to be quiet. It took time, but Janet was able to travel in peace with Stanley.

A dog who travels nicely in the car can be included on family outings and holidays.

Give some thought to where your dog can travel safely and comfortably.

a closer look at:
11. food-related problems

Again, this covers many difficulties, including:

- greedy dogs
- dogs who are not eating as much as they should
- stealing food
- aggression over food
- eating nonfood items.

Possible causes

There are many possible causes. The most likely one is simply being a dog!

Prevention and what to do if problems have arisen

Greedy dogs This a normal state for many dogs. If it seems excessive, speak to your veterinarian and perhaps consider a diet change.

Dogs who are not eating as much as they should The important thing is to know what is normal for your dog. If he generally leaves part of his food, this is usual for him. If a greedy dog starts to do this, this may signal a problem.

Stealing food A dog does not see this as a problem—it is normal dog behavior. In a pack situation, if food is available, it is up to the dogs to help themselves. Therefore, if food is within the dog's reach, do not be surprised if he helps himself. Put food away or out of reach if you feel your dog may be tempted.

Aggression over food Food is an important resource and some dogs guard their food if they feel threatened. It may be something he learned before you had him. The old remedy of taking the food away if the dog growls can make the situation much worse, and puts the owner at risk of being bitten. It is important that the dog learns to trust. Seek specialist advice.

Eating nonfood items If your dog eats nonfood items rather than simply chewing them, remember that just because it does not look like food to us, this may not be how your dog sees it. Some dogs eat tissues, stones, or more revolting things. See your vet if you are worried about anything you think your dog may have eaten.

Some dogs like to rip up and chew pieces of cardboard or paper. This kind of behavior should be monitored and gradually stopped.

• First, ensure safety. If your dog swallows something dangerous, an operation may be needed to remove it.

• Then seek veterinary advice to find out if the problem is physical, or perhaps due to a dietary deficiency.

• If all is well physically, decide if it is something you can live with, perhaps by avoiding the situations, or if you need to seek advice from a counselor.

In all instances, seek specialist help if the problem is severe or worrying to you.

Case History

Robbie

Robbie loved his food and also loved everyone else's. Mrs. Smith tried shouting at him each time he helped himself to her food. After a few repetitions, Mrs. Smith realized that this was not working. Robbie seemed confused and was beginning to be afraid of her whenever she walked into a room. In Robbie's mind, he could not understand his owner's reactions. Taking the food was highly rewarding, it tasted great! No one was around to stop him, so it must be all right, mustn't it? But then, some time later, Mrs. Smith would come into the room and be really annoyed. Robbie had no idea why. Just to make it more confusing, she would push the empty plate at him. When he licked it, she got even more cross. What was the problem? Mrs. Smith realized that she and Robbie saw things differently. Getting angry with him was not helping, so she began to be more careful with food. If she left the room, she made sure that food was out of Robbie's reach.

a closer look at:
12. attention seeking

In a dog's mind, any attention is better than none. Therefore, although they may prefer pleasant, positive attention, negative attention is better than being ignored. If sitting quietly results in no attention, but barking results in being told to shut up, many dogs will choose to bark. When we look at the situation from the dog's point of view, we can see that it is not surprising that they often learn behaviors we do not want.

Possible causes

Any unwanted behavior, including barking, jumping up, running around, pawing and stealing objects, can be caused by the dog learning that this is a good way of getting immediate attention.

Prevention

• Reward good behavior.

• Ignore unwanted behavior.

• It must be in the dog's best interests to behave in the right way.

• Make sure that your dog has plenty to occupy him, mentally and physically.

• For short periods of time each day, ignore your dog totally. Remember, ignoring means do not look at, talk to or touch him. If your dog is doing something that you cannot ignore, such as jumping on your knee, either gently move him off with no attention, or get up and walk out of the room, closing the door on him briefly.

Sometimes, the reward for unwanted behavior is obvious.

What to do if problems have arisen

• Look at what you are doing. Have you inadvertently rewarded the dog for doing this?

• Consider how you can change your reaction so that your dog gets what he wants—your attention—for doing what you want.

• If this does not work, or you are unsure about what you should be doing, seek expert advice.

This problem is especially seen in:

• clever, affectionate dogs who love their owners

• opportunistic dogs.

Case History

Sasha

Sasha was a bright, young dog. She loved her owner and enjoyed being with her. One evening, she was bored, so she picked up her toy and took it to Janet. Janet was engrossed in a soap opera and ignored Sasha, so Sasha tried another toy. Same result! Sasha looked around for inspiration and found Janet's purse. She picked it up and Bingo!, the reaction was immediate. "What have you got there?" shouted Janet, as

she chased Sasha around the house. What a great game, thought Sasha, the only thing is, make sure you don't get caught.

In the days that followed, Sasha practiced her skill until she learned what items would bring the best reaction from Janet. Whenever she wanted to be the center of attention, she would look around for these items and would then run away with them.

a closer look at:

13. excessive noise

This is one of the most common reasons for problems with dogs, but there is no single "cure." Why is your dog barking?

• Is he trying to get your attention?

• Is it when he is left alone?

• Is it at people, when he feels anxious?

• Is it when people come to the door?

We know he is barking, but what is he saying?

Find out why he is barking. Then read the appropriate section of the book.

Excessive barking, like attention seeking, can be something which has unwittingly been encouraged.

a closer look at:
14. chewing, mouthing, housebreaking

These are all behaviors shown by puppies, and many dogs learn the right behavior with no further problems. All are discussed earlier in the book.

However, occasionally problems persist and we must look at what we can do.

Chewing

There are several different causes for this.

• Age. Most chewing occurs when the dog is between 8 and 14 months of age. Be prepared for this and have plenty of safe items around for him.

• Attention seeking.

• Problems when the dog is left alone.

• Boredom or lack of stimulation.

Prevention

Make sure your dog has plenty to do. This includes mental and physical exercise with you, as well as things to do without you.

• Hold an interesting toy in one hand and an item such as the TV remote control in the other. Let your dog sniff them both. If he tries to chew the remote control, say "no" and wiggle the toy. As soon as he shows interest in the toy, praise him and play with him. Repeat at different

times with different objects. Then begin to leave different items around, for example drink coasters on a low table or the remote control on the seat of the sofa. Watch your puppy carefully. A quick sniff of the object is allowed, but if he begins to put his teeth around it, say "no" and gently move him away. See previous sections for more details.

Playing with and chewing the right items can help reduce chewing problems.

Mouthing

If this persists past puppyhood, why is your dog doing this?

• For your attention? Read the previous section.

• He wants his own way or to prove a point? Read the sections on your dog's position in the pack.

• It is his idea of a game? Make sure no one is playing rough games or any that encourage mouthing.

• He is excited? Calmly teaching your dog how to control himself will help—see the chapter on training. Ignore unwanted behavior and calmly reward good behavior.

• To avoid something, such as handling? Read the chapter on handling.

Case History

Digby

Digby came to his new home in the summer. Housebreaking seemed easy, Lyn just left the back door open all the time and Digby went out of his own accord. But when autumn arrived and the door was shut, Lyn was horrified to find that Digby started to soil in the kitchen. Although Lyn thought that Digby was housebroken, he had only learned that he preferred to go outside if given a choice. He did not understand that if access to outside is not available, he should hold himself or ask to go out. Once Lyn realized that Digby did not fully understand housebreaking and that he was not being naughty, she watched him carefully and rewarded him for waiting short periods. Within a couple of weeks, Digby was reliable in the house.

Housebreaking

If problems are persisting longer than you would expect, try to see the situation from the dog's point of view. Is he learning the wrong things?

Reread the previous section. Make a determined effort to work with your dog. Keep a close eye on him at all times. Do not give him the opportunity to make a mistake. As with everything, if problems are severe, persistent, or worrying, seek expert help.

Mouthing becomes more of a problem, as well as more painful, as a dog gets older.

a closer look at:
15. new baby in the home

The arrival of a new baby involves many changes that could lead to problems. With a little thought and effort, it is possible to make sure that stress and change is kept to a minimum for your dog.

Before the baby arrives

• Make any changes to your dog's routine now rather than waiting until the baby arrives. Does your dog sleep in the bedroom, jump on furniture, knees etc? Are you happy for him still to do this?

• Work out how your dog will still get his walks and quality time with you.

• Make sure that your dog is happy being shut out of the room as there will be times when he has to be.

• Play a tape recording of a baby crying so that your dog does not become upset when he hears the real thing.

• If you are uncertain about anything, seek advice.

Make sure that you have quality time with your dog and your baby, even in the early stages.

First introductions

If you have your baby in the hospital, it is likely that you will have been away from home for a couple of days.

• Therefore, on your return, have someone to wait outside with the baby, while you come in and greet your dog.

• When he has said hello, bring the baby in. Car seats are a great idea.

• It is a good idea to let your dog notice and investigate the new baby, if possible. Discourage any intimate licking!

• Reward good behavior.

Life with a dog and a baby

• Make sure that your dog still has as normal a routine as possible so he does not get anxious.

• Your dog still needs quality time with you. Whenever possible, try to do this when your new baby is around. If your dog learns that all good things happen when your baby is away, it is possible he will begin to resent the baby's presence.

• As your baby grows, make sure that your dog and your baby have good experiences together. Throwing treats is something many young children can do. Progress to games with toys, always under close supervision. Walks together and cuddle sessions all help the dog and child to learn how to enjoy being together.

• *Never* leave babies or young children alone with dogs.

• Do not allow your child to handle your dog roughly.

• Get your dog used to being handled more roughly by you. Small children pull, grab, and poke. Get your dog used to you doing this to him. (Do this when your child is not around to see. We do not want the child to learn this behavior and think that this is acceptable.)

Case History

Hal

When Jenny was expecting her first baby, she sought advice and read books about dogs and babies. When Charlie was born, he was her first priority, but her dog Hal's needs were also considered. Five years later, she has a second child and is closer to Hal than ever. She is home more than previously, the family have lots of trips, and Hal is included on most of them. Jenny appreciates the fact that Hal is the least demanding, least moody member of the family.

What to do if problems have arisen

If there are any signs about which you are unsure, seek expert help at once.

As a baby becomes mobile, a dog must learn to cope with the new situation. Supervision becomes even more essential since a crawling baby can frighten and even hurt a dog without meaning to.

a closer look at:
16. owning more than one dog

In today's society, many people choose to own more than one dog, the idea often being that this will be double the pleasure and half the work. However, this is not always the case. Owning two or more dogs can be extremely rewarding and enjoyable, but it should be considered at least three times the amount of work of owning one. Not only should you work with each dog individually, but you need to spend time teaching them what you expect when they are together.

If you have one dog who is reasonably mature and behaves as you would like, and you feel that you have the time, energy, and money for another dog, then go ahead and investigate the possibilities.

However, if you are considering a second (or subsequent!) dog for any of the following reasons, then do think very carefully.

• Your original dog is very energetic and you feel a second dog would give him someone to play with. If you do not have time for one dog, how are you going to have time for two of them?

• You leave your dog for long periods of time and feel another one would be company. Another dog is not a substitute for human involvement.

• You decide to take two puppies from the same litter. Teaching and socializing two puppies at once is extremely hard work.

• Your dog already shows some problems and you feel that a second dog may stop this. It is more likely that the second dog will copy, and you will then have two dogs exhibiting unwanted behavior.

Statistically, there are many more problems with second dogs than with first. When we acquire a dog, he has no option but to learn from us, play with us, and so on. We proudly take him out and about. When our second dog arrives, he has a choice, to learn either from the other dog, or from the people. Most dogs choose their own species. Therefore, it becomes harder to develop the same bond with the new dog. Socialization often receives a lower priority. Consequently he learns from the older dog and may develop unwanted habits. He is less willing to learn from his owner.

Owning two dogs can be twice as much fun, but it is more than twice as much work.

Steps must be taken to prevent this.
- Treat each dog as an individual.
- Spend time with each dog separately. This includes playing games, training sessions, and at least some walks. Once each dog understands what you want individually, begin doing things with both together.
- Make sure that the dogs spend quality time with you, not just with each other.
- Separate them at times in the house, perhaps letting them into the yard individually, or having one in a room with one family member and another somewhere else.
- Make sure that each dog can cope when away from the other.
- It is not a good idea for the same person in the family always to be involved with the same dog. If you want family dogs, all the family should be equally involved with each dog.

Do not be discouraged from owning more than one dog, but be prepared for the extra work and time involved.

If you frequently leave two dogs to entertain each other, do not be surprised if they learn some unwanted behaviors.

professional **advice**

Looking at the situation from the dog's point of view, it is not surprising that sometimes our dogs do not fulfill our expectations since they are quite high!

We expect so much more from our dogs in today's society that there is greater pressure than ever before for our dogs to behave well. In addition, we are more attached to our dogs and so unwanted behavior can have serious effects for us.

What is a behavior problem? This varies, since what one person may find difficult to live with may be acceptable in another household. Therefore, if *your* dog is showing any behavior with which you are unhappy, this would be termed a problem.

Make an appointment with a consultant or counselor before the problem behavior becomes entrenched and more difficult to resolve.

Do not feel ashamed or guilty about admitting that your dog's behavior is not always what you would want. Perfect dogs are few and far between and it is a sign of a caring and responsible owner to want to do all that is possible to insure problems are minimized.

It is not surprising that there is an increasing number of people offering help when things have not gone according to expectations. There are various titles for these people, and the service, fees and quality of service vary. Consultant or Counselor in Animal Behavior is one such term. At present, there are very few restrictions on who can do what, although this is likely to change in the future. Behavior specialists should not be judgmental. The old attitude of "there are no bad dogs, just bad owners" has been replaced by the more enlightened view that some dogs are a great deal more difficult than others and that we impose such an unnatural lifestyle on our dogs now that problems inevitably arise.

Very often a consultation with a behavior specialist is seen as a "last resort." This often means that:
• the problem is now more difficult to resolve
• the problem has become an established habit
• some of the attempts to resolve the problem may have made the situation worse
• the owners are generally so fed up that they have neither the time nor the energy to work at the problem.

Seeking help early means that there is a far better chance of the problem being resolved more easily.

How do you find help?
The first step is to speak to your veterinarian if you are beginning to get worried about certain aspects of your dog's

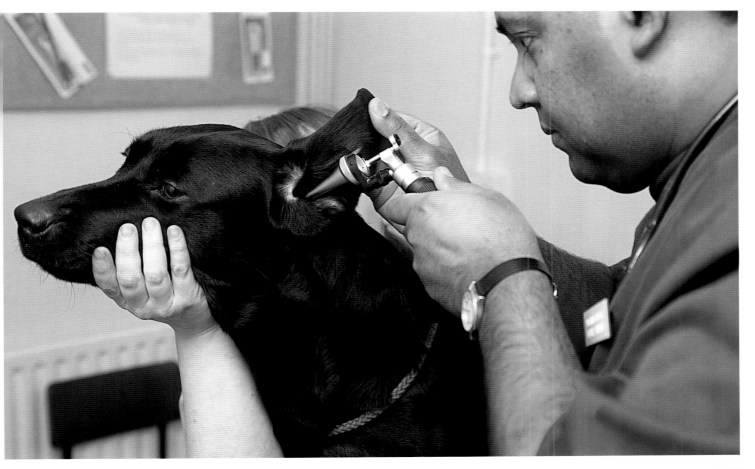

Your veterinarian can check your dog to find out if anything medical is causing or contributing to the problem. He will be able to help or refer you to a behavior specialist.

behavior. Discuss the situation and ask your vet to check your dog to make sure that there is nothing physical causing or contributing to the unwanted behavior. The veterinarian should then be able to discuss the options with you.

Most reputable behavior specialists will only work on veterinary referral, following a veterinary checkup, so be prepared for this.

Life Skills

Choosing a Specialist

If you are considering a consultation with someone, check:
• their reputation. Your veterinarian should know this.
• their own experience and qualifications. This must be relevant to what you want. You need to be sure that the person has the correct combination of theoretical knowledge and practical experience.
• their membership of a reputable body. Although this is not essential, if a person is a member of an official behavior organization, it is likely that they have been assessed or accredited and fulfill certain criteria.

What should you expect from your consultation?

First, it is not a magic wand. You are unlikely to see instant changes in your dog's behavior. Changes come about through hard work and commitment, for which you must be prepared.

You will be asked to make some changes to your daily routine. You cannot continue as before and expect your dog to change his behavior. You are likely to need to change yours first. When discussing a behavior modification plan, suggestions should be realistic and practical. Success will depend on you. However, you should be able to acquire support over the telephone following the consultation. A consultation is likely to last between one and a half and two hours. This allows for a thorough history to be taken, with time for discussing an individual program. It is helpful for all the family to be present, since everyone should be involved. If this is not practical, it is essential that everyone is committed to working with the dog and sits down to discuss the plan following the consultation.

Learning the right social behavior as a puppy means that dogs are less likely to develop problems later in life.

Be realistic. Some problems can be cured while others can only be lessened and the situation improved.

Some counselors work by visiting you in your own home, others expect you to travel to them or to a clinic.

How many visits would I expect?

This varies according to the nature of the problem and also the way in which the counselor works. Find out before committing yourself.

Many counselors provide one or maybe two consultations, with follow-up help over the telephone. If subsequent sessions would be beneficial, this could be arranged, or you could be referred to a specialist class.

Fees

Fees will vary considerably, along with the service offered. Bear in mind that you will be consulting a professional, who has had considerable study and experience.

It is also worth remembering that many veterinary insurance policies will cover fees charged by certain behavior counselors.

Dog classes

Many dog classes cater for pet dogs and teach general manners and education for dogs. Most do not have the facilities to offer specialist, individual help with problem situations. Resolving a behavior problem may need individual help with a person specializing in this. Having said this, a good class can provide a controlled environment for setting up situations for gradual introductions to dogs or people. It is possible that your dog would not be ready for this during the initial stages, but would benefit as you progress with the behavior modification plan.

Rehabilitation classes

These are classes run by specialist trainers who have developed an interest and furthered their knowledge of dogs exhibiting specific problem behaviors. Classes would normally be very small, so that each dog would receive plenty of individual attention. These rehabilitation classes can give huge support to owners and provide a safe environment for those who are working through a behavior modification program. Entrance into the class would normally be after a consultation, either with the trainer or with a behavior counselor. These classes are tremendously helpful in certain situations, but although they are gaining in popularity, there are still not enough to assist everyone who has problems.

People who are qualified and experienced can help you to help your dog.

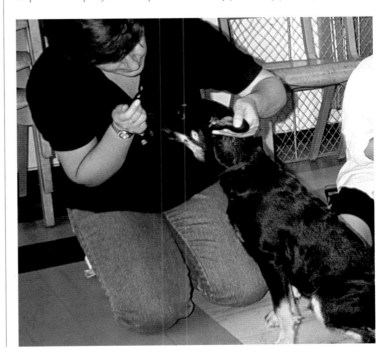

drug therapy
and alternative treatment

Is there a magic pill that will cure a behavior problem? No, unfortunately, there is not.

The idea of medication to help resolve a behavior problem is an emotive area. Some people would love to be able to give a tablet to their dog and do very little else, others feel that they would prefer to avoid drugs, because of possible side effects.

There are very few drugs licensed for treatment of behavior problems. The ones that do exist clearly state that they are to be used in addition to a behavior modification program, not instead of.

Life Skills

Making the Right Choice

No tablet can teach your dog how to behave. As most behavior problems arise because the dog has learned the wrong behavior or not learned the right behavior, medication cannot give him this knowledge. However, there are instances when medication can help the dog to be in the right frame of mind to enable learning to take place more quickly. In these instances, medication can be an option and should be discussed with your behavior counselor and also with your veterinarian.

The first step should always be a consultation with your veterinarian. A behavior counselor should then work with you, and your veterinarian where relevant. Sometimes, there is a link with a physical problem which it may be possible to resolve, with or without drug support. Even if this is the case, the dog may have learned some unwanted behavior that may persist as a habit. This is when behavior therapy is essential.

There is also a range of alternative treatments available. Their effects are varied. Treatment would range from over-the-counter remedies to a consultation with a specialist, such as a homeopathic veterinarian.

Homeopathic remedies have helped to achieve success with dogs exhibiting unwanted behavior. Herbal remedies and flower remedies have been used with great success with some dogs and are generally available over the counter. Read any literature that you can get hold of. However, there are people who have studied these more deeply and so a consultation with a trained therapist may be more beneficial.

Touch therapy is a way of touching your dog which many dogs and owners find helpful. This can be learned and put into practice by owners, whereas a skill such as acupuncture is far more specific and does require a qualified practitioner.

Aromatherapy is also proving beneficial in some instances. Consult a local practitioner for information.

As with conventional drug support, a behavior modification program in tandem with another therapy would need to be followed to be sure of the best results. Remedies alone cannot teach your dog what you want or rebuild a bond that has deteriorated.

In order to find out more about any alternative treatments, ask your own veterinarian and also read the dog magazines for articles and advertisements. These types of treatments are now more widely available as they become more broadly accepted.

Some people have strong views about drug and alternative treatments. The important thing is to know what is available, enabling you to make your own choice about what is best for you and your dog.

Touch therapy and different forms of massage can be beneficial to dogs with sore joints or just as a calming measure.

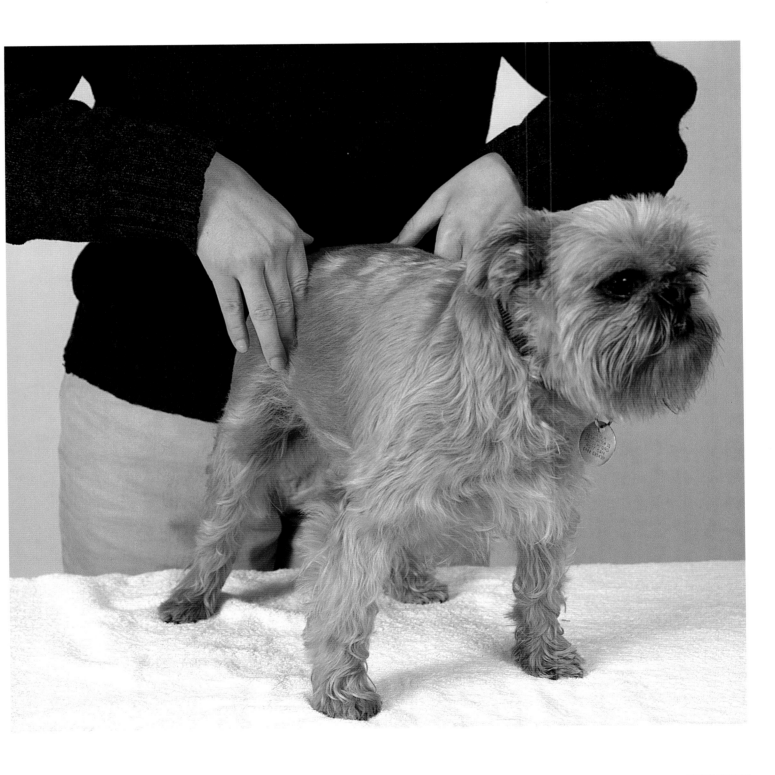

conclusion

The reality of dog owning can be very different from the image that is generally presented in films and books. Our dogs are not "mini-humans." They cannot understand human values and make judgements that we always feel are right. However, they have their own abilities, which we must learn to understand, appreciate, and perhaps channel into acceptable outlets.

We choose to own dogs and we get pleasure from this. However, there are times when owning a dog can be less of a pleasure than it should be. Sometimes this is unavoidable. Walking in the cold and wet and then having to dry your dog at the end can be less than ideal but, overall, owning a dog should be enjoyable for dog and family.

The better we understand our dog, the closer our relationship can become. Preventing problems becomes easier and life with our dog becomes more enjoyable.

Hopefully, this book has helped you towards achieving this happy and balanced relationship.

You are the expert on your own dog, so get to know him. If you feel that any of the suggestions here are not appropriate for your dog, do not follow them. If you feel that something you are doing is not right for your own dog, stop doing it. You must do what you feel most appropriate.

No book can provide all the answers. Your dog is unique and what you want from him is not necessarily what someone else would want. Therefore, if this book has whetted your appetite, take the opportunity to pursue this interest further. You and your dog will both benefit.

Always bear in mind:

• Put your own point of view aside. Try to think from your dog's point of view.

• Do not expect to understand everything, we cannot ever fully understand what it is like to be a dog. However, the more that we do understand, the closer we can become and the more rewarding our relationship is with our pet.

• Remember your dog's own instincts since this will alter his motivations and perceptions of life. Some of these will arise because he is a dog, some will be influenced by his particular ancestry.

• Do not forget that you choose to own your dog, not the other way around. Therefore, be prepared for the hard work that dog owning entails, as well as the rewards.

• Avoid labels such as "naughty" or "disobedient." Instead, try to work out why he is exhibiting a certain behavior. From here, decide what you can change to help him understand what you want.

• Do not expect instant changes. In most instances, good results are the culmination of dedication and persistence. Many behaviors are habits that have been present for some considerable time. It is not easy to change these.

• Watch your dog and learn from him.

• Be consistent at all times.

• Be nice to your dog, we are all on the same side!

• Reward all good behavior.

• Have fun. Enjoy your dog, and make sure he enjoys you.

glossary

Aggression. This means different things to different people. In dogs, it generally means any action or display that implies the intent to hurt another at some stage during the interaction.

Animal behavior counselor. One of several terms that is used to describe a person who works with a family in order to help resolve the unwanted behavior of a pet. Animal behavior counsellors should normally have relevant qualifications and experience, working only on veterinary referral.

Chaining. A method of teaching a complicated exercise. The exercise is broken into small segments and each segment taught separately, before putting it all together, when each segment then becomes the trigger for the next.

Dog dictionary. A list of words which the owner has taught, or is teaching, the dog to respond to. This helps everyone to be more consistent.

Habituation. The process of becoming accustomed to new situations/environments/objects through exposure. This is particularly applicable to puppies.

Housebreaking. The process of teaching a dog or puppy to eliminate only in appropriate areas, generally outside, not inside.

Hyperactivity. The exact definition is complex in the human world, where it means a syndrome, a combination of symptoms. Most owners use it to mean that their dog is more active or energetic than they would like.

Ignore. Ignoring a dog means to act as though he is not there, to refuse to take notice of him. This means not looking at the dog, not talking to him, not touching him.

Mouthing. In the pet dog world, mouthing refers to the behavior of a dog or puppy chewing or biting hands, feet, and clothing. This is commonly seen in puppies but occasionally persists if the dog is not taught that it is unacceptable. This is not the same as biting in an aggressive way, but mouthing can lead to biting. In obedience and gundog work, mouthing can refer to the undesirable habit of the dog chewing an article while retrieving.

Puppy class. This is normally a course of lessons for puppies, usually as soon as their vaccination program is completed or when their veterinarian is happy for them to attend. The classes should aim to teach the basics of puppy education.

Puppy party. Most often, these are held at veterinary premises. Very young puppies and their families are invited, normally before the vaccination process is completed. It gives the puppies the opportunity to have good experiences with other puppies and people and in the veterinary premises at a time when they would normally have to be isolated.

Rehabilitation class. These classes are run by a behavior counselor or trainer with specialist training. Classes are designed to help families with dogs exhibiting certain problem behavior. This means that dogs can be around other dogs or people in a controlled situation in order to help work on the unwanted behavior.

Reverse chaining. *See* Chaining. Reverse chaining is similar, but the last segment is taught first, then the next to the last, etc. This process makes it easier for an animal to learn what you want him to do.

Reward. In this context, a reward is something the dog wants which comes as a result of his actions.

Shaping. A method of teaching complex responses where the reward is given for successive approximations toward the desired response.

Situational learning. The phenomenon whereby animals associate learning predominantly with the environment where they were taught This includes dogs who behave differently in the church hall, during dog lessons, or a dog who only responds when the owner is standing at the side of him.

Socialization. The process of learning the right behavior through pleasant experiences when meeting new people, dogs, etc. This is particularly applicable to puppies.

Release word. A word or short phrase such as "OK" or "go play," which signals to the dog that the exercise is over and he can now move or go off and do his own thing.

useful addresses

American Kennel Club
260 Madison Avenue
NYC 10016
Tel: (212) 696-8200
email: publiced@akc.org
Website: http://www.akc.org

American Pet Association
P.O. Box 7172
Boulder CO 80306-7172 Tel:
(800) 272-7387
Website:
http://apa@apapets.org

**American Society for the
Prevention of Cruelty to
Animals (ASPCA)**
424 92nd St
NY 10128
Tel: (212) 876-7700
Website: http://www.aspca.org

**Association of Pet Dog
Trainers**
P.O. Box 3734
Salinas CA 93912-3734
Tel: (408) 663-9257
Website: http://www.apdt.org

**American Animal Hospital
Association**
P.O. Box 150899
Denver. CO 80215-0899
Tel: (303) 986-2800

**American Boarding Kennels
Association**
4575 Galley Road, 400A
Colorado Springs, CO 80915
Tel; (719) 591-1113
Website: http://webs.abka.com

**National Association for
Professional Pet Sitters**
6 State Road (113)
Machanicsburg PA 17050 Tel:
(717) 691-5565
Website:
http://apa@apapets.org

**The national and regional
offices of the Humane
Society of the United States,
and the states they serve:**

**The Humane Society of the
United States (DC, MD &
VA)**
2100 L Street, NW
Washington, DC 20037
Tel: (202) 452-1100
Website: http://www.hsus.org

**Central States Regional
Office (IL,KY, MN, NC, TN,
WI)**
800 West 5th Avenue,
Suite 110 Naperville, IL 60563
Tel: (630) 357-7015

**Great Lakes Regional Office
(IN, MI, OH, WV)**
745 Haskins Street
Bowling Green,
OH 43402-1696
Tel: (419) 352-5141

**Mid-Atlantic Regional
Office (DE, NJ, NY, PA)**
Bartley Square, 270 Route 206
Flanders, NJ 07836
Tel: (973) 927-5611

**Midwest Regional Office
(IA, KS, MO, NE)**
1515 Linden Street
Suite 220 Des Moines,
Iowa 50309
Tel: (515) 283-1393

**New England Regional
Office (CT, MA, ME, NH,
RI)**
Route 112, Halifax Jacksonville
Town Line
Mailing address: P.O. Box 619
Jacksonville, VT 05342-0619
Tel: (802) 368-2790

**Northern Rockies Regional
Office (AK, ID, MT, ND,
SD, WY)**
490 North 31st Street,
Suite 215 Billings, MT 59101
Tel: (406) 255-7161

**Southeast Regional Office
(AL, FL, GA, MS, SC)**
1624 Metropolitan Circle,
Suite B, Tallahassee, FL 32308
Tel: (850) 386-3435

**Southwest Regional Office
(AR, AZ, CO, LA, NM, OK,
TX, UT)**
3001 LBJ Freeway,
Suite 224, Dallas, TX 75234
Tel: (972) 488-2964

**West Coast Regional Office
(CA, HI, NV, OR, WA)**
5301 Madison Avenue,
Suite 202
Mailing address: P.O. Box
417220, Sacramento,
CA 95841-7220
Tel: (916) 344-1710

acknowledgements

The author and publishers would like to thank the following for their generous participation in the photography for this book:

Kendal
nine-week-old bull mastiff

Martin and Ann Chipchase
HALEWOOD VILLAGE
LIVERPOOL, UK

Molly
eight-week-old labrador

Elizabeth Hanpson
WALLASEY, UK

Sally
sixteen-week-old bearded collie

Mrs. Janice Roe-Evans
MEOLS
WIRRAL, UK

Millie & Mollie
sixteen-week-old crosses

Dorothy More
WHISTON
KNOWSLEY, UK

Bailey
fifteen-week-old-cocker spaniel

Janet Taylor
HEATHFIELD
CALBY, UK

Banrhilna
sixteen -week-old german shorthaired pointer

Jo Tyrell
WEST KIRBY, UK

Billy
fouteen-week-old west highland terrier

Helen Fitzpatrick
MEOLS, UK

Jake
twenty-week-old german shepherd dog

Mal Hattersley
WEST KIRBY, UK

Odin
seven-year-old english mastiff

Mrs. Bernthal
FLINTSHIRE
NORTH WALES

Corey
seven-year-old-cross

M Spiden
NEW BRIGHTON
MERSEYSIDE, UK

Claude
two-year-old hungarian pooley

Paul Plant
WALLASEY
WIRRAL, UK

Rhea
six-year-old gordon setter

Abbey
two-year-old king charles cavalier

Lillian Weston
BROMBOROUGH, UK

Molly
six-month-old golden retriever

Liz Roberts
NEWTON
WEST KIRBY, UK

Benji
two-year-old king charles cavalier

Lynne Myerscough
NEWTON
WIRRAL, UK

Jamie
three-year-old west highland terrier

Mrs Harris
PORT SUNLIGHT VILLAGE
WIRRAL, UK

Emi
seven-month-old parson jack russell

Maureen Wright
GREASBY WIRRAL, UK

Millie
one-year-old cross

Roz Staveley-Taylor
WEST KIRBY, UK

Hera
nine-year-old cross

Frank Peachey
WEST KIRBY
WIRRAL, UK

Fudge
three-year-old stafford cross whippet

Richard Shillcock
UPTON
WIRRAL, UK

Mollie
six-month-old cocker spaniel

Mrs. F. Pitchford
WHITBY, UK

Remus
two-year-old german shepherd dog

Mrs Lees
HIGHER BEBINGTON
WIRRAL, UK

Hebe
two-year-old jack russell

Francesca Clarke
SLINFOLD
HORSHAM
SUSSEX, UK

Elsa
fifteen-year-old cross

Heidi
eight-year-old cross

Lorena Bedford
FLINT
FLINTSHIRE, UK

All the staff, especially Richard Moore at the National Canine Defence League, Merseyside

index